P9-DFP-188

HIDDEN MICKEYS

• •

A Field Guide to

Walt Disney World®'s

Best Kept Secrets

• •

4th edition

Steven M. Barrett

The INTREPID TRAVELER

HIDDEN MICKEYS

A Field Guide to Walt Disney World®'s
Best Kept Secrets
4th edition

Published by
The Intrepid Traveler
P.O. Box 531
Branford, CT 06405
http://www.intrepidtraveler.com

Copyright ©2009 by Steven M. Barrett
Fourth Edition
Printed in Canada
Cover design by Foster & Foster
Interior Design by Starving Artist Design Studio
Maps designed by Evora Taylor
Library of Congress Control Number: 2009922203
ISBN-13: 978-1-887140-84-3

10 9 8 7 6 5 4 3 2 1

Trademarks, Etc. ●●●●●●●●●●●●●●

Photo by Vickie Barrett

About the Author............

Author Steven M. Barrett paid his first visit to Disney World in the late 1980s, after attending a medical conference in Orlando. He immediately fell under its spell, visiting it twice yearly with family and friends for the next several years, offering touring advice to the less initiated, and reading almost everything written about the WDW theme parks. When a job in his field of emergency medicine opened up not far from WDW in 1998, Barrett, a Texas native, Air Force veteran, and former Oklahoma City medical professor, relocated to the Orlando area from Houston, Texas. He began visiting the WDW parks every chance he got to enjoy the attractions, sample the restaurants, and escort visiting friends and relatives. Eventually, their feedback made him realize he had better advice on touring the parks than they could get anywhere else. So he wrote the guidebook *The Hassle-Free Walt Disney World® Vacation*, which includes customized touring plans for adults and teens, families with younger children, and seniors, along with lots of insider tips gleaned from his almost weekly visits to WDW. His interest in Hidden Mickeys led him to take pen in hand once again. This book is the result.

Dedication...................

I dedicate this book to my wife Vickie and our son Steven, who willingly accompanied me on countless research visits to Disney World and added invaluable insight to this book. Furthermore, updating this book would not be possible without the many wonderful Hidden Mickey fans I've met through my website and in the Disney parks. Thanks to you all.

True to their name, Hidden Mickeys are elusive. New ones appear from time to time and some old ones disappear (see page 21). When that happens — and it will — Steve will let you know on his web site:

www.HiddenMickeysGuide.com

So if you can't find a Mickey — or if you're looking for just a few more — be sure to check it out.

Table of Contents . . . .

Maps

Acknowledgements ....

No Hidden Mickey hunter works alone. While I've spotted most of the Hidden Mickeys in this book on my own — and personally verified every single one of them — finding Hidden Mickeys is an ongoing group effort. I am indebted to the following dedicated Hidden Mickey lovers for alerting me to a number of Hidden Mickeys I might otherwise have missed. Thanks to each and every one of you for putting me on the track of one or more of these WDW treasures and, in some cases, also helping me verify them. Extra special thanks to Sharon Dale for spotting over 200 Hidden Mickeys and to Jesse Kline for finding over 100 of the elusive gems!

Names in bold have spotted 10 or more. You can find each person's contribution(s) by visiting my website, www.HiddenMickeysGuide.com.

Candi A., Maxine A., Nancy A., Frank Abbamonte, Debbie Acres, Kaitlyn Rae Adams, Ron Adams, Sarah Adams, Nancy Ahlsen, Michael Akers, Lindsey Albrecht, Anthony Almeyda, Jordan Altug, Cathy Ames, John Ames, Amy Amyot, Michelle Anderson, Robert Anderson, Kristin Archibald, Mark and Dean Ashwaite, Michelle Astuti, Barb B., Dan B., Devon B., Jason B., Jessica B., Andrew Babb, Sarah Bagwell, Salina Barbosa, Steven Madison Barrett, Vickie Barrett, Chris Barry, Diana Barry, Diane Barry, Samantha Barry, Nicholas Bartoli, Johnny Bartolomeo, **James Baublitz**, Sarah Baywell, Penny and Jeff Beam, Brittany and Craig Bedelyon, Jonathan Beer, **Annmarie and Josh and Rick Benavidez**, Rich Benneau, Richard Bent, Clark Benton, Jeffrey Berg, Patti Berg, Bryan and Stacy and Jenna Berger, **David and Celia Berset**, Jenny Bess, Tom Binder, Andy Birkett, Murray Bishop, Roberta Blackburn, Mark Blackie, **Erin Blackwell**, Louis Blanco, **Nancy Blevins**, Laurie and Rebecca Bloodworth, Jennifer Bogdan, Rich Bonneau, Michael Bonnett, Jr., Kevin Booton, Storie Borgman, Katie Borland, Craig Boudreaux, Wendy Bowen, the Bowles family, Donna Brackin, Brent Brandon, Tina Brannen, Todd Breakey, Matthew Brennan, J. Bridge, Christine Bristow, Daniel Brookwell, Stephen Brookwell, Jaye Brown, Jeff Brown, Karen Brown, Peter Brown, Roberta Brown, the Brown family, John and Susan P. Bruederle, Paul Brune, Erica Bryant, the Buaas family, Earl Burbridge, Nancy Burke, Lisa Burleson, Jon Bushee, Ruth Butler, Giovanni C., Villa Cadlle, Bret Caldwell, **Peter Caldwell**, Sarah Callanan, Anne Campbell, Lisa Campbell, Craig Canady, Jason Cannons, Stan Carder, Chris Carlson, Gary Carr, Alexis Cavileer, Christina Cella, Kelly Challand, J. Chappa, Julie Chappa, Catherine Chiarello, Dana Christos, Alyssa Ciaccio, Vito Ciaccio, Anne-Marie L. Clanton and family, Matthew Clemons, Malcolm Cleveland, Alexa Cohen, Serena Cohen, Rob Coile, Elizabeth Coler, John Coliton, Greg Conlin, Colin Kevin Connor, Joey Connors, Jeffrey Contompasis, Lindsay Contreras, Colleen Costello, Calvin Cotanche, Angela Coutavas, Sara Cox, George Crippen, Rob Croskery, Kasie Culp, Erica Culver, Nancy Curl, Curtis D., Katie D., Marie and Bruce Daigneault, **Sharon and Chloe Dale**, Christina Darce, Jim Darling, Christopher Dash, Bob Decker, Keenan DeFrisco, Bethany and Christine DeLaurentis, Dwayne Degler, Robert Delgado, Mike Demopoulos, Stephen DeSanto, Rich DeTeresa, **Tim Devine**, Dania Dewese, James Dezern, the DiBenedetto family, Cara Di Cicco, Doug Dillard, James and Jennifer DiMaggio, Max Dinan, Sam Dinan, Calvin Dolsay, Gina Dorkins, Laura Dubberly, James Duggan, Joey Duggan, Tom Durr, Abby Dwyer, Alex Dwyer, Ian Dwyer, John Early, Jason Ebels, Susan Edgington, Erik Edstrom, Seth Edward, Nicholas Elardo, M. Eldred, Amber Ellis, Eric England, Kelly and Kimberly Erickson, Nick Exley, Eric Fabian, Nick Falco, Adam Fanjoy, Ken Fanti, Ronald and Gianna Fazio, Joshua and Krystina Fears, Alan and Craig Fergus, Kathy Fetters, Dom Fiandra, Elaine Finnigan, Dennis Flath, Sharon Flood, Jessica Flowers, Dave Flynn, Stephanie Foley, Melissa Forbes, Joseph Fortenbaugh, Joe Franceschino, Sr. and Joe Franceschino, Debbie Frazier, Eden Frazier, Matt Freeman, Devon Friedman, Rachel Friedman, Ryan and Fairen Frisinger, Jake Fruci, Diane Furtado, Jason Gall, Justine Gamale, Brad Garfinkel, Marilyn Garfinkel, Scott Garland, Tony Garon, Kristen Gartrell, Pauline Gibson, Kaela and Ryan and Jake Gilbert, Mark Goldhaber, Nathan Goley, Jeremiah Good, Ty Goode, Andrew Goodwill, June Goodwill, William Goodwill, Trevor Goren, James and Edward Goring, Ryan Goukler, Josh Graham, Tim Grassey, Mark Greenwald, Rick Gregg,

9

Bill Griffin, Robert Grohman, Ryan Gutzat, Chris and Cindy H., Christine H., Cindy H., Rick Haas, Brandi Hall, Byron Hall, Melanie Hall, Mike Hamilton, Shannon Hamilton, Theresa Hamway, Donna Hardter, Ray Harkness, Bernice Hasher, Laura and Ross Haston, Bryan Hauser, Ed Harriger, Abby Hawthorne, Colin Healy, Mary Heidenberg, Kurt Heinecke, Claudia and Ralph Hemsley, Brian Henry, Otto Hernandez, Louise Herrick, Ricky Hett, Jamie Lee Hindes, Jim Hines, Joan Hinkle, Matt Hochberg, Rick Hoefinghoff, Ed Hoffman, Paul Hoffman, Chip Holland, Vivian Holland, Joyce Holroyd, Jamie Holz, Evelyn Horton, Kim Howe, Erik Hubbard, Emily and Lynette Huey, Elton Hughes, Brennan Huizinga, William Huntley, Cameron Hutt, **Bill and Donna Iadonisi**, Dawn and Megan Ilsley, the Ilsley family, Mike Ireland, Ashley Izzo, Andy Jackson, Mark Jackson, Andy Jasinski, Mark Jeffries, Jessica Johnson, Trisha Johnson, Samantha and John and Brian Jonckheere, Laura Jones, the Jones family, Tim Jones, Michelle June, Michael Kania, Gary Kaplow, Debbie Karnes, Ray Kastner, Constance Katsafanas, Brent William Kee, Aaron and Evan Keller, Gayle Keller, Jennifer Keller, Robert Keller, Melanie Kemper, the Kemper family, Deb Kendall, Jasmine Kennedy, John Kessel, Brian Keys, Sam Kimport, Bonnie King, James King, Rachel Kirk, Maggie Kirkwood, Rochelle Klay, Aaron Klein, Cheryl Klein, Patty and Patrick and Adam and Megan Klein, Paul and Michelle Klein, Mitchell Michini Klepac, **Jesse and Jordan Kline**, Jordan Kline, John Koerber, Deb Koma, Gloria Konsler, Wendy Kraemer, Tim Kress, Chris Kretzman, Austin Kruckmeyer, Mikey Laing, Kim Lamb, Anne Langlotz, Brian Lanier, Meris Larkins, Dick Larson, Tim Larson, Rebecca Lawler, Daniel Lawson, Russell Le Blanc, Will LeBlanc, Joshua Lehrer, Becca Leipzig, Justin Lemonds, Lisa Leonard, Jennifer Leone, Angie Leslie, Billy Lewis, Bradley Lewis, Luke Licygiewicz, Taricia Lightfoot, Kyle Lighting, Beth Lindemann, Chuck Lionberger, J. Loesch, Christie Long, Marc Lorenzo and son, John Lovett, Stephen Lovelette, Ashley Lowe, Nick Lowman, Jennifer Lynch, Jim Lyon, Will Lyon, Linda Mac, Chris Macri, Cholle Madere, Dusty Madere, Hope Madere, Karen Madere, Mason Madere, Shane Madere, Beci Mahnken, John Majcherek, Austin Malone, Katherine Manetta, Sharla Manglass, Kristy Mantarro, Frank Marando, John and Stephanie Marshall, Drake

Martin, Jeffrey Martin, Breanne Martine, Brian Mart-
solf, James Massoni, Pam May, Allison and Andy
Mayo, Greg Mazzella, Kelly McAdams, Mark Mc-
Curry, Chris McDaniel, Mark McDonald, Chris Mc-
Donnell, Jessica McGilvary, Saffron McGregor, Billy
and Zoe McInerney, Andrea McKenna, **Donna Mc-
Murrey**, Allissa McNair, Michala McNair, JerriAnne
and Susan McPherson, Jill Meadows, Joseph Mehr,
Amy Mentz, Brian Mentz, Sharon Meyer, Kim Mich-
aux, H. Mildonian, Geoff Miller, Rich Miller, Todd and
Jennifer and Sean Miller, Patti Minden, Sandy Modes-
itt, Aruna Mohan, Perry Molinoff, Kelly Monaghan,
Lou Mongello, Michelle Moody, Jennifer Moon, Sha-
ron Moore, Mickey Morgan, the Moriarty family, Rick
Morin, Joseph Moschinger, Phil Motto, Scott Mueller,
the Muklewicz family, Ed Muller, Brodie Mumphrey,
Marty Murray, Brenda N., L. Naizer, Kurt Nank, Mi-
chael Nemeroff, Brayson Nesbitt, Mandy Newby, Jeff
Newcomb, Mary Newell, Victoria Newhuis, Benjamin
and Aden Newman, Darrin Nilsson, Joe Nixon,
Cheryl Nutter, Andrew and Matthew Nypower, Denise
O., George O'Brien, Steve Okeefe, Jeff Oldham, Da-
vid Oliver, Giovanni Oliveras, Beth Olliges, Bob
Ondercik, Bobby Ondercik, Rita Ondercik, Sheri
Ondercik, Susie Ondercik, A. O'Neill, Lisa O'Reilly,
Orlando Attractions Magazine, Greg Ostravich, the
Outra family, Denise Owen, Annette Owens, Charles
Owens, Curtis P., Kristin P., Melissa P., Glenn and
Vickie Pacheco, Bill Padonisi, Doreen Pakidis, Jessica
Paneral, Benoit Paquin, Nancy Paris, Caleb Parry, Cal-
ley Pate, Bob and Maryellen Paton, Chad and Megan
Paton Evans, Sam and Kimberly Paton Vegter, Brian
and Drew Patterson, Kyla and Jen Patton, Jonathan
Peczinka, Tawny L. Peedin, Natalie Pence, Todd Perl-
mutter, Caleb Perry, Jenny Perry, John Perry III, John
Perry IV, Sheila Peters, Kristina Peterson, Lucy Peterson,
Tony and Kara Peterson, Steve Petty, Patrick Phelan,
Martin Pierce, Victoria Pike, Brooke Pimental, Linda
Pinto, Susan Pitts, Linda Pizzuro, Amanda Plante,
Krista Porter, Roberta Powers, Al Prete, Karen and
Grace Price, Katherine Price, Kirby Price, Nathan
Price, Walt Prindle, Hayden Pronto-Hussey, Matt Pucci,
Todd Pushman, Erica R., Tessa R., Tim Rachuba, Rich-
ard Rando, Nicholas Ranger, Carol Ray,
Sharon Reedy, Stacy Reedy, Derrick Rees,
Lynne Reilly, Johnny and Jyle Reis, Michael
Remy, Kathy Riccardi, Chris Ricci, Nik Ricci,

11

Mikey Ricco, D. Richmond, Brian Rigsby, Antonio Riquelme, Jose Riquelme, Rob and Kathy Risavy, Joy E. Robertson-Finley, Andy and Jay and Angel Robey, Joseph Robinson, Lawrence Robinson, Lawrence Robson, Terry Rohrer, Robyn Romine, Emily Rose, Matt Roseboom, Timothy Rowe, Mitch Rozetar, Chris Rudolph, James Rudolph, Jim Rudolph, Shauna Rupert-Sessions, Ed Russell, Christine Russo, Steve Russo, Heather S., Steve S., Robin Sackevich, I and Y Sakurada, Andy Salerno, Tami Sanker, Christina Santoro, Andrew Savers, Dee Dee Scarborough, Jackie Scheibis, Josh Schickler, Julie Schneider, Sherrie Schoening, Hank Schultz, Spencer Schweinfurth, Bethany and Michael Scibetta, Carol Scopa, Mike Scopa, Jeri Scott, Keira Scott, Todd Seales, Steve Seifert, David and Aubree Serkoch, Trent Sexton, Khrys Sganga, Leslie Sharkey, John Sheehan, Randy Shelton, Bob Shoemaker, Bret Shortall, Stephanie Shultz, Scott Siblovin, Scott Sigouin, Deb Silhan, Tyler Silhan, Stephen Simmons, James Simon, **James Sisson**, Bridget Skallet, Mike Sluss, Byon Smiddy, Laura Smiley, Bonnie Smith, Neil Smith, Michele Snoddy, Benjamin Soto, Roy Souders, Kitty Spangler, Megan Spellman, Ryan Spellman, Steve Spevak, Michele Sponagle, Megan Stallings, Michael and Emily Steele, Kevin Stein, Joshua Steiner, Sharon Stevenson, Mark Sties, Skip and Susan and Jack Stinson, Heather Stone, Jay Stonefield, Branson Strawderman, the Suarez family, Jill Sullivan, David Sutton, Dan Swain, Jordan and Kenya Swiss, Joey Sylvester, Kathy Szczerba, Jen T, Jenni Tackett, Alex Taday, Karen Taylor, Len Testa, Samantha and Mikayla Tewksbury, Alayna Theunissen, Kimmie Thomas, Brian Thompson, Jake Thompson, Laura Thompson, Albert Thweatt, Erin Tickno, Paige Tiffany, Martha Tischler, Kristy and Scott and Jim and Kim Todd, Frank Tonra Jr., Frank Tonra III, Kevin Toomey, Whitney Townsend, Lauren and Steven Tracy, Kendra Trahan, Marcel Troost, Beverley Tuck, Brandon Tucker, Glenn Turner, Terry Ulrich, Melissa Uzzilia, Nicole V, Stephen Valente, Max-Emanuel Vingerhoets, Aninka van Staden, Frank van Wijk, Tairyn Velie, Fred Vosecky, Deven Wagenhoffer, Maureen Wahtera, Harry Walker, Jeanne Walker, Amanda Wallace, the Walsh family, Jonathan Ward, Rachel Ward, Sharon Ward, Dena Weber, Rebecca Webster, Scott Weideman, Fred Weiner, Cheri Weitkamp, Carrie Welf, Matt Wells, John Weyrich, Craig Wheeler, John Wheeler, Shona Whiddon, Jennah and Noah Whitcomb, Jeff Whitlock, Katarina Whitmarsh, Sharon Whitney, Patricia Whitson, Becky Williams, Carla Williams, Chris Williams, Jason Williams, Kevin Williams, Scott Williams, Susan Williams, Ida Williamson, Garret Willis, Deb Wills, Amory Wilson, Debbie Wilson, Jeannette Winner, Darren Wittko, Harry Wootan, Elizabeth Worth, Kassidy and Cody Wright, Lynn Yaw, Callum Young, Heather Young, Meghann Zanotta, Kristine Zolciak, Catherine Zori, and Aaron, Aimee, AJ, Al, Alan, Alexis, Alison, Allie, Allison, Alyssa, Amy, Andy, Ann, Anonymous, Austin, Benjamin, Beth, Blair, Brad, Brad & Courtney, Brandon, Brian, Brianne, Brooke, Bryan@allaboutthemouse.com, Caitlin, Caitlyn, Catherine, Charlene, Charles, Charlotte, Chloe, Christopher, Christy, Claudia, Colin, Colleen, Courtney, C.T., Darren, Dave, David, Denise, Devon, Donna, Eloy, Emily, Emma, Eric, Erik, Evan, Foxx, Gen, Gilbert, Giovanni, Graffix, Greg, Hidden Kid, Hidden Mickster, Hoffman, Jackie, Jake, Jake of Lake Mary, Jamie, Janelle, Jason (TrendyMagic), JB Jeanette, JE.D, Jennah, Jennifer, Jeremy, Jessica, Jodi and Nana and Pops, Joe, Jonathan, Joseph, Josh, JP and son, Julie, Jyl, Katie, Kelly, Kelma, Ken, Keri, Kerri, Kimberly, Kimmie, Kira, Kitzzy, Kristin, Kyle, Laura and Joe, Lauren, Laurie, Lea, Lea Ann, Luis, Lyinel, Lynn, Maria, Marissa, Matthew, Max, Megan, Melissa, Michael, Michelle, Mike, Natalie, Nick, Nickole, Noah, Patti, Quinten, Rick, Rikki, rjf1423, Roman, Rumbanana, Sarah, Shannon, Sharon, Sharon from Auburn, Skiyalater, Someone, Sonali, Stacey, Stephanie, Taricia, Taylor, Tim, Toontownkid4, Tricia, Trina, Tyler, Vicki, Victoria, Zach, and Zachary.

Read This First! . . . .

My guess is that you have visited Disney World before, perhaps many times. But if I've guessed wrong, and this is your first visit, then this note is for you.

Searching for Hidden Mickeys is lots of fun. But it's not a substitute for letting the magic of Disney sweep over you as you experience Walt Disney World (WDW) for the first time. For one thing, the scavenger hunts I present in this book do not include all the attractions in WDW. That's because some of them don't have Hidden Mickeys! For another, this book doesn't cover many things the first-time visitor should know and do to make that first trip to Disney World as magical as possible.

So for first-time visitors (and repeat visitors looking for a way to experience the attractions with less hassle), I recommend my guide, *The Hassle-Free Walt Disney World® Vacation*. It contains up-to-date, customized touring plans for adults and teens, families with young children, and seniors, along with descriptions of all the WDW attractions, tips for planning your vacation, WDW restaurant ratings, and coverage of the WDW Resort hotels. You'll find it in bookstores or on the Web at IntrepidTraveler.com.

That doesn't mean you can't search for Hidden Mickeys, too. Just follow the suggestions in Chapter One of this book for "Finding Hidden Mickeys Without Scavenger Hunting."

Hidden Mickey Mania

● ●

Have you ever marveled at a "Hidden Mickey"? People in the know often shout with glee when they recognize one. Some folks are so involved with discovering them that Hidden Mickeys can be visualized where none actually exist. These outbreaks of Hidden Mickey mania are confusing to the unenlightened. So let's get enlightened!

Here's the definition of an official Hidden Mickey: a partial or complete image of Mickey Mouse that has been hidden by Disney's Imagineers and artists in the designs of Disney attractions, hotels, restaurants, and other areas. These images are designed to blend into their surroundings. Sharp-eyed visitors have the fun of finding them.

The practice probably started as an inside joke among the Imagineers (the designers and builders of Disney attractions). According to Disney guru Jim Hill (www. JimHillMedia.com), Hidden Mickeys originated in the late 1970s or early 1980s, when Disney management wanted to restrict Disney characters like Mickey and Minnie to the Magic Kingdom. The Imagineers designing Epcot couldn't resist slipping Mickey into the new park, and thus "Hidden Mickeys" were born. Guests and "Cast Members" (Disney employees) started spotting them and the concept took on a life of its own. Today, Hidden Mickeys are anticipated in any new construction at Walt Disney World, and Hidden Mickey fans can't wait to find them.

Hidden Mickeys come in all sizes and many forms. The most common is an outline of Mickey's head formed by three intersecting circles, one for Mickey's round head and two for his round ears. Among Hidden Mickeys fans, this image has been known as the "classic" Hidden Mickey, a term I will adopt in this book. Other Hidden Mickeys include a side or oblique (usually three-quarter) profile of Mickey's face and head, a side profile of his entire body, a full-length silhouette of his body seen from the front, a detailed picture of his face or body, or a three-dimensional Mickey Mouse. Sometimes just his gloves, handprints, shoes or ears appear. Even his name or initials in unusual places may qualify as a Hidden Mickey.

And it's not just Mickeys that are hidden. The term "Hidden Mickey" also applies to hidden images of other popular characters. There are Hidden Minnies, Hidden Donald Ducks, Hidden Goofys, and other Hidden Characters in Disney World, and I include many of them in this book.

The sport of finding Hidden Mickeys is catching on and adds even more interest to an already fun-filled Walt Disney World vacation. This book is your "field guide" to more than 800 Hidden Mickeys in WDW. To add to the fun, instead of just describing them, I've organized them into six scavenger hunts, one for each of the major theme parks, one for the Walt Disney World Resort hotels, and one for all the rest of WDW: the water parks, Downtown Disney, WDW Speedway, and beyond. The hunts are designed for maximum efficiency so that you can spend your time looking for Mickeys rather than cooling your heels in lines. Follow the Clues and you will find the best Hidden Mickeys WDW has to offer. If you have trouble spotting a particular Hidden Mickey (some are extraordinarily well camouflaged!) you can turn to the Hints at the end of each scavenger hunt for a fuller description.

Scavenger Hunting for Hidden Mickeys

To have the most fun and find the most Mickeys, follow these tips:

★ **Arrive early** for the theme park hunts, say 30 minutes before the official opening time. Pick up a Guidemap and a Times Guide and plot your course. Then look for Hidden Mickeys in the waiting area while you wait for the rope to drop. You'll find the clues for those areas by checking the *Index to Mickey's Hiding Places* in the back of this book. Look under "Entrance areas." If you arrive later in the day, you may want to pick up a

FASTPASS for the first major attraction and then skip down a few clues to beat the crowds.

★ "Clues" and "Hints"
Clues under each attraction will guide you to the Hidden Mickey(s). If you have trouble spotting them, you can turn to the Hints at the end of the hunt for a fuller description. The Clues and Hints are numbered consecutively, that is, Hint 1 goes with Clue 1; so it's easy to find the right Hint if you need it. In some cases (*Test Track* in Epcot is a notable example), you may have to ride the attraction more than once to find all the Hidden Mickeys.

★ Scoring
All Hidden Mickeys are fun to find, but all Hidden Mickeys aren't the same. Some are easier to find than others. I assign point values to Hidden Mickeys, identifying them as easy to spot (a value of 1 point) to difficult to find the first time (5 points). I also consider the complexity and uniqueness of the image: the more complex or unique the Hidden Mickey, the higher the point value. For example, some of the easy-to-spot Hidden Mickeys in Mickey's Toontown Fair in Magic Kingdom are one-point Mickeys. The brilliantly camouflaged Mickey hiding in the Garden Grill Restaurant mural in Epcot is a five-pointer.

★ Playing the game
You can hunt solo or with others; competitively or just for fun. There's room to tally your score in the guide. Families with young children may want to focus on one- and two-point Mickeys that the little ones will have no trouble spotting. (Of course, little ones tend to be sharp-eyed; so they may spot familiar shapes before you do in some of the more complex patterns.) Or you may want to split your party into teams and see who can rack up the most points (in which case, you'll probably want to have a guide for each team).

Of course, you don't have to play the game at all. You can simply look for Hidden Mickeys in attractions as you come to them (see "Finding Hidden Mickeys Without Scavenger Hunting," below).

★ Following the clues
The hunts often call for crisscrossing the

parks. This may seem illogical at first, but trust me, it will keep you ahead of the crowds. Besides, it adds to the fun of the hunt and, if you're playing competitively, keeps everyone on their toes.

★ Waiting in line

Don't waste time in lines. If the wait is longer than 15 minutes, get a FASTPASS (if available and you're eligible), move on to the next attraction, and come back at your FASTPASS time. Exception: In some attractions, the Hidden Mickey(s) can only be seen from the queue line, and not from the FASTPASS line. (I've not suggested FASTPASS in the Clues section when that is the case.) The lines at these attractions should not be too long if you start your scavenger hunt when the park opens and follow the hunt clues as given. If you do encounter long lines, come back later during a parade or in the hour before the park closes. Alternatively, use the singles line if available.

★ Playing fair

Be considerate of other guests. Many Hidden Mickeys are in restaurants and shops. Ask a Cast Member's permission before searching inside sit-down restaurants, and avoid the busy mealtime hours unless you are one of the diners. Tell the Cast Members and other guests who see you looking around what you're up to, so they can share in the fun.

Finding Hidden Mickeys Without Scavenger Hunting

If scavenger hunts don't appeal to you, you don't have to use them. You can find Hidden Mickeys in the specific rides and other attractions you visit by using the *Index to Mickey's Hiding Places* in the back of this book. For easy lookup, attractions in Magic Kingdom and Disney's Animal Kingdom are also listed under their appropriate "lands" (for example, Fantasyland in Magic Kingdom and Asia in Animal Kingdom). In Epcot, attractions are listed alphabetically and by pavilion. To find Hidden Mickeys in the attraction, restaurant, hotel or shop you are visiting, turn to the *Index*, locate the appropriate page, and follow the Clue(s) to find the Hidden Mickey(s).

Caution: You won't find every WDW attraction, restaurant, hotel or shop in the Index. Only those with confirmed Hidden Mickeys are included in this guide.

Hidden Mickeys, "Gray Zone" Mickeys, Wishful Thinking

The classic (three-circle) Mickeys are the most controversial, for good reason. Much debate surrounds the gathering of circular forms throughout Walt Disney World. The large classic Hidden Mickey outlined in the cement at the rear of Africa in Disney's Animal Kingdom (Clue 90 in the Animal Kingdom Scavenger Hunt) is surely the work of a clever artist. However, three-circle configurations occur spontaneously in art and nature, as in collections of grapes, tomatoes, pumpkins, bubbles, oranges, cannonballs, and the like. Unlike the cement Hidden Mickey in Africa, it may be difficult to attribute a random "classic Mickey" configuration of circles to a deliberate Imagineer design.

So which groupings of three circles qualify as Hidden Mickeys as opposed to wishful thinking? Unfortunately, no master list of actual or "Imagineer-approved" Hidden Mickeys exists. Purists demand that a true classic Hidden Mickey should have proper proportions and positioning. The round head must be larger than the ear circles (so that three equal circles in the proper alignment would not qualify as a Hidden Mickey). The head and ears must be touching and in perfect position for Mickey's head and ears.

On the other hand, Disney's recent mantra is: "If the guest thinks it's a Hidden Mickey, then by golly it is one!" Of course, I appreciate Disney's respect for their guests' opinions. However, when the subject is Hidden Mickeys, let's apply some guidelines. My own criteria are looser than the purists' but stricter than the "anything goes" Disney approach. I prefer to use a few sensible guidelines.

To be classified as a real classic Hidden Mickey, the three circles should satisfy the following criteria:

19

1. Purposeful (sometimes you can sense that the circles were placed on purpose).

2. Proportionate sizes (head larger than the ears and somewhat proportionate to the ears).

3. Round or at least "roundish."

4. The ears don't touch each other, and the ears are above the head (not beside the head).

5. The head and ears touch or are close to touching.

6. The grouping of circles is exceptional or unique in appearance.

7. The circles are hidden or somewhat hidden and not obviously décor (decorative).

Having spelled out some ground rules, allow me to now bend the rules, in one instance. Some Hidden Mickeys are sentimental favorites with Disney fans, even though they may actually represent "wishful thinking." (My neighbor, Lew Brooks, calls them "two-beer Mickeys.") Who am I to defy tradition? For example, the "three-gears classic Mickey" at *Big Thunder Mountain Railroad* in the Magic Kingdom is not proportioned quite right and so is a bit of a stretch. But many guests and even Cast Members call the gears a Hidden Mickey, and I'll admit, I rather like it myself. So you will find it in the Magic Kingdom Scavenger Hunt in Chapter 2, Clue 3.

Hidden Mickeys vs. Decorative Mickeys

Some Mickeys are truly hidden, not visible to the tourist. They may be located behind the scenes, accessible only to Cast Members. You won't find them in this field guide, as I only include Hidden Mickeys that are accessible to the guest. Other Mickeys are decorative; they were placed in plain sight to enhance the décor. For example, in a restaurant, I consider a pat of butter shaped like Mickey Mouse to be a decorative (aka décor) Mickey. Disney World is loaded with decorative Mickeys. You'll find images of Mickey Mouse on items ranging from manhole covers, to laundry room soap dispensers, to toilet paper wrappers and shower curtains in the hotels. I do not include these ubiquitous and sometimes changing images in this book unless they are unique or hard to spot.

Hidden Mickeys can change or be accidentally removed over time, by the process of nature or by the continual cleaning and refurbishing that goes on at Disney World. For example, the "Steamboat Willie" Hidden Mickey in the star map in Mickey's Star Traders shop disappeared when the shop was remodeled. Cast Members themselves sometimes create or remove Hidden Mickeys.

My Selection Process

I trust you've concluded by now that Hidden Mickey Science is an evolving specialty. Which raises the question, how did I choose the more than 800 Hidden Mickeys in the scavenger hunts in this guide? I compiled my list of Hidden Mickeys from all resources to which I had access: my own sightings, friends, family, Cast Members, websites, and books. (Cast Members in each specific area usually — but not always! — know where some Hidden Mickeys are located.) Then I embarked on my own hunts, and I took along friends or family to verify my sightings. I have included only those Hidden Mickeys I could verify.

Furthermore, some Hidden Mickeys are visible only intermittently or only from certain vantage points in ride vehicles. I don't generally include these Mickeys, unless I feel that adequate descriptions will allow anyone to find them. So the scavenger hunts include only those images I believe to be recognizable as Hidden Mickeys and visible to the general touring guest. It is likely, though, that one or more of the Hidden Mickeys described in this book will disappear over time.

I'll try to let you know when I discover that a Hidden Mickey has disappeared for good by posting the information on my website:

21

www.HiddenMickeysGuide.com

If you find one missing before I do, please email me care of my website to let me know.

I have enjoyed finding each and every Hidden Mickey in this book. I'm certain I'll find more as time goes by, and I hope you can spot new Hidden Mickeys during your visit.

So put on some comfortable walking shoes and experience Walt Disney World like you never have before!

Happy Hunting!

— *Steve Barrett*

Magic Kingdom Scavenger Hunt

Clue 1: Examine the scrollwork of the roof of the Main Street Train Station.
2 points

★ While you are waiting for the park to open you may want to hunt for Hidden Mickeys on **Main Street, U.S.A.** (See clues 161 to 174.)

★ Cross the park to Frontierland and get a FASTPASS to ride *Splash Mountain* later. Then ride **Big Thunder Mountain Railroad**.

Clue 2: During the first climb, search the cavern floor to the right of the coaster.
4 points

Clue 3: Look for a classic Hidden Mickey on the ground to your right near the end of the ride.
2 points

Clue 4: Study the reddish rock along the exit walkway for a Hidden Tinker Bell.
4 points

★ Return to **Splash Mountain** at your allotted FASTPASS time. Hop aboard and keep your eyes peeled for a Hidden Mickey in the queue, six on the ride and at least three more after you exit.

Clue 5: Along the queue, concentrate to your left for a red Mickey hanging on the wall.
3 points

Clue 6: Just as your boat goes outside, spot a tiny classic Mickey on a "moonshine" barrel!
5 points

Clue 7: Soon after you start, search for barrels that form a classic Mickey.
3 points

23

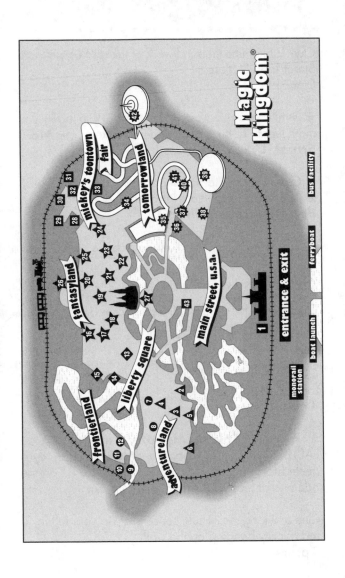

CHAPTER 2: MAGIC KINGDOM SCAVENGER HUNT

1 WDW Railroad, Entrance

adventureland

2 Swiss Family Treehouse

3 The Enchanted Tiki Room Under New Management

4 The Magic Carpets of Aladdin

5 Jungle Cruise

6 Pirates of the Caribbean

frontierland

7 Frontierland Shootin' Arcade

8 Country Bear Jamboree

9 Splash Mountain

10 WDW Railroad

11 Big Thunder Mountain Railroad

12 Raft to Tom Sawyer Island

liberty square

43 The Hall of Presidents

44 Liberty Square Riverboat

45 The Haunted Mansion

fantasyland

16 "it's a small world"

17 Peter Pan's Flight

18 Mickey's PhilharMagic

19 Cinderella's Golden Carrousel

20 Dumbo the Flying Elephant

21 Snow White's Scary Adventures

22 Fairytale Garden

23 The Many Adventures of Winnie the Pooh

24 Mad Tea Party

25 Pooh's Playful Spot

26 Ariel's Grotto

27 Castle Forecourt Stage

mickey's toontown fair

28 Minnie's Country House

29 Toontown Hall Of Fame

30 Mickey's Country House

31 WDW Railroad

32 Donald's Boat

33 The Barnstormer at Goofy's Wiseacre Farm

tomorrowland

34 Tomorrowland Indy Speedway

35 Stitch's Great Escape!

36 Monsters, Inc. Laugh Floor

37 Buzz Lightyear's Space Ranger Spin

38 Galaxy Palace Theater

39 Walt Disney's Carousel of Progress

40 Tomorrowland Transit Authority

41 Astro Orbiter

42 Space Mountain

main street, u.s.a.

43 Guest Information Board

25

Clue 8: Just past Brer Frog, find the fishing bobbers that form a Hidden Mickey.
4 points

Clue 9: In the room with jumping water, spot the hanging rope classic Mickey.
4 points

Clue 10: As your boat ascends toward the big drop, look toward the opening for a side profile of Mickey's face.
3 points

Clue 11: In the riverboat scene after the big drop, find the Hidden Mickey in the clouds.
4 points

Clue 12: Along the exit walkway, look for the birdhouse with at least two acorn classic Mickeys.
3 points for two or more

Clue 13: Search for the Hidden Mickey in the children's play area at the exit.
3 points

Clue 14: After the ride, take another look at the mountain from the outside viewing area to spot that side profile (again).
3 points

★ Walk into Adventureland. Ride the ***Pirates of the Caribbean*** and find 14 classic Hidden Mickeys.

Clue 15: Along the left entrance queue, look near a faux fireplace for a Hidden Mickey.
5 points

Clue 16: Search for two classic Mickey locks in the left queue.
4 points for spotting both

Clue 17: Along the left queue, spot some cannonballs.
3 points

Clue 18: When Davy Jones appears on the ride, look up for a classic Mickey.
5 points

Clue 19: Try to spot the classic Mickey shadow above the drunken pirate's cat.
4 points

Clue 20: As you approach the bridge, study the pirate with the dangling leg.
5 points

Clue 21: Near the end of the ride, look left at the recessed doors in the wall.
4 points

Clue 22: Check out the lanterns.
5 points

Clue 23: Don't miss the treasure room's open door.
4 points

Clue 24: Now glance at the wall behind Jack Sparrow.
4 points

Clue 25: As you exit the ride, search for some coins and jewels.
5 points for all

Clue 26: In a small camera shop near the *Pirates* ride, look around for a classic Mickey.
3 points

★ Take a short break and grab some refreshment in Frontierland or Liberty Square, which has a good fruit stand. Afterward: Stop by the **Frontierland Shootin' Arcade**.

Clue 27: Find a classic Mickey in front of the target area.
1 point

★ Then turn right to **Liberty Square** and cross the street.

Clue 28: Find the classic Mickey at the *Liberty Square Riverboat* entrance.
1 point

★ Head for **The Haunted Mansion**. (Get a FAST-PASS if the wait is too long.) Find six classic Mickeys, two Donald Ducks, and a Mr. Toad!

Clue 29: In the first room inside the entrance, look for some classic Mickeys in the border design around a portrait.
3 points

Clue 30: During the ride, be alert for Donald Duck on two different chairs.
4 points each

Clue 31: Find the Mickey on the ghostly banquet table.

2 points

Clue 32: Spot plates on the floor in the attic.
4 points

Clue 33: Look closely at the "grim reaper" by the opera singing lady.
5 points

Clue 34: Along the exit hallway, stare at the ceiling for a Mickey image.
3 points

Clue 35: Outside, as you exit, look for a classic Mickey next to a gate.
3 points

Clue 36: Find Mr. Toad along the exit walkway.
3 points

★ Enter the **Columbia Harbour House** restaurant and look for a classic Hidden Mickey. (Be considerate of the diners.)

Clue 37: Check the art on the downstairs walls.
2 points

★ Now cross the bridge to Tomorrowland and go to the **Tomorrowland Indy Speedway**.

Clue 38: Look for a shadow on the pavement near the *Speedway* that's shaped like a classic Mickey.
3 points

★ Enjoy an early lunch (around 11:00 a.m.) to avoid the crowds. Suggestions: The Plaza Restaurant off Main Street for sit-down or Cosmic Ray's Starlight Café in Tomorrowland for chicken or burgers.

★ After lunch, walk to **Mickey's Toontown Fair**. (Note: Some Hidden Mickey hunters might consider most of the Mickeys in this area décor Mickeys, rather than Hidden Mickeys. But they are such fun to pick out that I've included many of them in the hunt.)

Clue 39: Keep your eyes peeled as you walk through the street.
1 point

★ Go to **Minnie's Country House**.

Clue 40: Spot the Mickey on the outside chimney.
3 points

★ Now step inside Minnie's house.

Clue 41: Look for classic Mickeys on the wall in the first room.
3 points

Clue 42: A small, side-profile Mickey is somewhere in the second room.
3 points

Clue 43: Search for tiny classic Mickeys along the right wall of the second room.
5 points

Clue 44: Find yellow and blue classic Hidden Mickeys in Minnie's sewing room.
1 point for yellow
1 point for blue

Clue 45: Stare high for Mickey ears.
2 points

Clue 46: Spot Mickey ears in the hallway to the kitchen.
3 points

Clue 47: Don't miss a classic Mickey clasp in the hallway to the kitchen.
3 points

Clue 48: Look for ceramic Hidden Mickeys.
3 points for spotting two types

Clue 49: Find a classic Mickey on a table.
1 point

Clue 50: Observe the pots and pans in Minnie's kitchen to find another classic Mickey.
1 point

Clue 51: Spot a classic Mickey in the fridge.
2 points

Clue 52: Look up for two classic Mickeys in a cabinet.
2 points for spotting both

★ Stroll over to **Mickey's Country House**. Mickey's house and garden are loaded with Hidden Mickeys: Try to find 25 Mickeys plus a hidden Donald Duck and a Hidden Goofy.

Clue 53: Find four classic Mickeys on the way in.
1 point each

Clue 54: There's one in Mickey's bedroom.
1 point

Clue 55: Spot two more on the wall outside the bedroom.
1 point each

Clue 56: Search below the mirror for one.
3 points

Clue 57: Take a look at the fence in the next room.
1 point

Clue 58: Study the table in the living room.
3 points

Clue 59: Now find two classic Mickeys, a Donald, and a Goofy in the game room.
2 points each

Clue 60: Find a side-profile Mickey in the kitchen.
4 points

Clue 61: In the kitchen, look for a classic Mickey on the wall.
3 points

Clue 62: Look around in the kitchen for a full-body Mickey.
2 points

Clue 63: Find two classic Mickeys just inside the second window of the kitchen.
5 points for spotting both

Clue 64: Explore Mickey's backyard (behind his house) and find at least three classic Mickeys in the bushes and plants.
1 point each; 3 points for three or more

Clue 65: Don't miss the rock Mickey in the backyard!
4 points

Clue 66: Look for Mickey on the back of a pole in the backyard.
4 points

Clue 67: Find a classic Mickey handle in the backyard.
3 points

Clue 68: Check the walls and shelves of Mickey's garage for two Hidden Mickeys.
1 point for the wall Mickeys
2 points for the table Mickey

★ Now check out the **Judge's Tent** to earn some possible bonus points.
1 bonus point for each HM you spot.

★ Cross over to **Donald's Boat**. (Watch out for the random water spurts!)

Clue 69: Search for Donald and Daisy Duck.
4 points for spotting both

★ Go to **The Barnstormer at Goofy's Wiseacre Farm**. (You can skip the main ride if you want.)

Clue 70: Along the entrance queue, find the Hidden Mickey near the silo. Psst! It's a side profile.
2 points

Clue 71: Inside the entrance queue barn, look up for tiny classic Mickeys in flight.
4 points

Clue 72: Outside the barn, search for a Hidden Mickey near the right fence.
3 points

Clue 73: Check out a classic Mickey on a sign near *The Barnstormer* entrance.
3 points

Clue 74: Stroll into the County Bounty Store and look around for Mickey on a merchandise stand.
2 points

★ Walk to **Tomorrowland** and get a FASTPASS for *Buzz Lightyear's Space Ranger Spin*.

Clue 75: Spot the classic Mickey on the FASTPASS machine.
2 points

★ Go to the outside of the **Monsters, Inc. Laugh Floor**.

Clue 76: Find the moon with classic Mickey craters.
1 point

Clue 77: Spot the asteroid shaped like a classic Mickey.
1 point

32

Clue 78: Get in line for *Monsters, Inc.*

Laugh Floor. As you enter the waiting area, search for a classic Mickey in a window display.
4 points

★ Go to **Walt Disney's Carousel of Progress** (open seasonally and on busy holidays). Check the third scene for Clue 79 and the last scene for the rest of the Clues.

Clue 79: Search for Mickey's blue hat.
4 points

Clue 80: Observe a painting on the rear wall.
4 points

Clue 81: Find a Mickey nutcracker.
2 points

Clue 82: Spot a Mickey Mouse doll.
2 points

Clue 83: Search around for green Mickey ears.
4 points

Clue 84: Look fast for a classic Mickey on a spaceship.
5 points

Clue 85: View an object with Mickey ears in the kitchen.
3 points

Clue 86: Don't miss Hidden Mickeys along the exit walkway.
2 points

★ Go to **Buzz Lightyear's Space Ranger Spin** at your allotted FASTPASS time and be on the lookout for nine Hidden Mickeys.

Clue 87: Inside the building on the right wall, find the planet with a continent shaped like the side profile of Mickey Mouse.
2 points

Clue 88: Look for this same planet further along the entrance queue to the left.
2 points

Clue 89: Search for a Hidden Mickey in Sector 2 nearby.
3 points

Clue 90: During the first part of the ride, spot another side profile of Mickey. Look to the left of your vehicle in the room with batteries.
3 points

Clue 91: Catch another view of the planet with Mickey in the space video room.
3 points

Clue 92: Just past the space video room, look straight ahead to spot that Mickey planet one more time.
2 points

Clue 93: Along the exit, look for an alien pointing to a classic Mickey.
2 points

Clue 94: Spot Stitch's spaceship nearby.
3 points

Clue 95: Search for two classic Mickeys in a star field.
4 points for spotting both

★ Walk to the far side of **Astro Orbiter** and search carefully for a small classic Mickey traced in the cement nearby.

Clue 96: Check the side facing *Space Mountain*.
5 points

★ Walk to **The Hall of Presidents**.

Clue 97: In the waiting room for the show, study the paintings for a tiny classic Mickey.
4 points

★ Go to the **Liberty Square Riverboat** (it sometimes closes at 5:00 p.m. or at dusk). If the wait is 10 minutes or more, grab a snack from a vendor in Liberty Square or Frontierland and refresh yourself while you wait to ride the boat.

Clue 98: From the boat, look for a classic Mickey rock formation at the right end of the bridge in Frontierland. (Note: This Hidden Mickey is also visible from *Tom Sawyer Island*.)
4 points

★ Watch the **afternoon parade** (usually 3:00 p.m.) wherever it fits in your schedule.

Clue 99: Search for Hidden Mickeys on the initial parade banner and on the Grand Marshal's car.
5 points for more than one

Clue 100: Look for classic Mickeys on the first float.
3 points

Clue 101: Scan both sides and the rear of the afternoon parade floats to find these Hidden Mickeys: a classic near a piano; a statue of Walt Disney and Mickey; an etched photo of Walt Disney.
5 points for all three

Clue 102: Don't miss the classic Mickeys on the final parade banner!
2 points

★ To see all the Hidden Mickeys, you need to look at both sides of some floats. So once the Pinocchio float passes you in Frontierland, go to **the far side of Main Street** by way of Adventureland to see the other side of the Pinocchio float and the rest of the parade.

★ From near *Big Thunder Mountain Railroad*, float on the raft over to **Tom Sawyer Island**.

Clue 103: Search one of the caves for Goofy.
3 points

★ Head for **Fantasyland**. Check out the waiting times for *The Many Adventures of Winnie the Pooh, Snow White's Scary Adventures,* and *Peter Pan's Flight.* Get a FASTPASS for *Peter Pan's Flight* or *Winnie the Pooh* (if available), then ride the other two if the waits are 20 minutes or less. Search for Hidden Mickeys as you go.

If the waits are long, return to enjoy these rides during an evening parade or in the hour before park closing.

★ Try to find five Hidden Mickeys as you enjoy **Snow White's Scary Adventures**. Look for the first two in the mural in the loading area.

Clue 104: Find a red classic Mickey on the Dwarves' laundry.
3 points

Clue 105: Look for three gray stones that form another classic Mickey.
2 points

Clue 106: During the ride, look closely behind the Wicked Queen to find a classic Mickey.
1 point

Clue 107: Pay attention to the turtle shell!
3 points

Clue 108: Then keep your eyes peeled for Mickey Mouse dressed as a Dwarf.
4 points

★ Go to **Peter Pan's Flight** (or return during—or after—your FASTPASS window).

Clue 109: Study the overhead attraction sign at the entrance for two decent Mickey images.
5 points for spotting both

Clue 110: Just before you get to the entrance queue turnstile, look closely at the bark of the trees facing the loading area to find a classic Hidden Mickey.
3 points

Clue 111: As your ship takes off, stare down to your right for a Hidden Mickey on a table.
4 points

Clue 112: Keep looking down for a brown classic Mickey on the ground.
5 points

Clue 113: Search for a classic Mickey near the mermaids.
3 points

★ Ride **The Many Adventures of Winnie the Pooh** (or return during—or after—your FASTPASS window) and look for five Hidden characters.

Clue 114: Examine the flower pot marker in Rabbit's Garden.
3 points

Clue 115: In Owl's house, find the picture of Mr. Toad and Owl.
3 points

Clue 116: Near the end of Owl's house, locate a picture of Mole with Winnie the Pooh.
3 points

★ See **Mickey's PhilharMagic** or get a FASTPASS to enjoy it later if the wait is too long.

Clue 117: In the first waiting area inside, squint at the wall mural.
4 points for two or more

Clue 118: Inside the main theater, examine the border of the video screen.
2 points

Clue 119: Look for a shadow Mickey on a table.
4 points

Clue 120: Stare at Ariel's jewels for a classic Mickey in a ring.
5 points

Clue 121: During the show, keep alert for a classic Mickey during the magic carpet ride.
5 points

Clue 122: Don't miss a classic Mickey along the exit walkway.
2 points

Clue 123: Stop in the gift shop at the exit and find a classic Mickey.
3 points

★ Enter **The Pinocchio Village Haus** restaurant.

Clue 124: Look for a tiny, dark classic Mickey on the wall near the exit to the restrooms.
4 points

Clue 125: Keep searching on this wall for a tiny, white classic Mickey.
5 points

★ Stroll over to **Fairytale Garden**.

Clue 126: Find a classic Mickey on a light pole.
3 points

Clue 127: Search for a Hidden Character on a wall.
4 points

★ Go to **"it's a small world"** and try to spot three classic Hidden Mickeys:

Clue 128: In the Africa room, look up at the vine with purple leaves.
3 points

Clue 129: Study the South America room for a classic Mickey on the floor.
3 points

Clue 130: In the South Pacific Room, search for an animal classic Mickey.
3 points

★ As you exit, head toward **Peter Pan's Flight**.

Clue 131: Find grapes arranged like a classic Mickey.
2 points

★ Stroll into **Pooh's Playful Spot**.

Clue 132: Search for a Mickey made of rocks embedded in the tree.
3 points

Clue 133: Look for a submarine image in the wood of the tree. (Tip: This is a hidden tribute rather than a Hidden Mickey.)
4 points

Clue 134: Find a side profile of Mickey in the bark.
4 points

★ Walk over to **Sir Mickey's Store**.

Clue 135: Observe a classic Mickey outside the store.
1 point

★ Stop near **The Yankee Trader** shop.

Clue 136: Look down at the hoofprints.
4 points

Clue 137: Now look around the Square for a tiny Hidden Mickey on a shopping stand.
4 points

★ Walk into **Ye Olde Christmas Shoppe**.

Clue 138: Spot a stack of logs with a Hidden Mickey.
2 points

★ Enter the **Frontier Trading Post** store in Frontierland.

Clue 139: Look for two rope classic Mickeys.
3 points for spotting both

Clue 140: Spot a cowboy with a Hidden Mickey.
3 points

★ Head for Adventureland. Pick up a FASTPASS for *Jungle Cruise*, if available. Then go see **The Enchanted Tiki Room – Under New Management**.

Clue 141: Find classic Mickeys at the bottom of two bird perches, one in the left

corner as you enter and the other in the right corner as you exit.
3 points each

Clue 142: Near the entrance to *The Enchanted Tiki Room*, look around for a Hidden Mickey on a statue.
3 points

Clue 143: Study the cement for a tiny classic Mickey between the Agrabah Bazaar shop and the *Magic Carpets of Aladdin* ride.
4 points

★ Eat an early dinner either before or after riding *Jungle Cruise*. One choice: The Crystal Palace buffet. Disney characters visit your table there, but priority seating reservations are usually needed unless you're both early and lucky.

★ Ride **Jungle Cruise** during your FASTPASS window and search for two Hidden Mickeys and two Hidden Donalds.

Clue 144: Watch for Donald Duck's face on a canoe.
4 points

Clue 145: Stay alert for a Hidden Mickey on an airplane.
4 points

Clue 146: Search the side of the river for Donald Duck's face on a native.
4 points

Clue 147: Coming out of the temple, look hard at the first undecorated column on the left for a chipped area of brick that forms part of a profile of Mickey's head and face. (This is a tough one!)
5 points

★ Walk through the **Swiss Family Treehouse**.

Clue 148: Keep alert for Mickey on the tree trunk.
5 points

Clue 149: Spot a Hidden Mickey at dinner.
3 points

★ Now cross the park to Tomorrowland and go to **Tomorrowland Transit Authority**. Find a Hidden Mickey as you ride.

Clue 150: In the last part of the ride, observe the accessories of the woman getting her hair done.
3 points

★ Walk to the **Merchant of Venus** shop.

Clue 151: Find a classic Mickey on a wall mural.
2 points

Clue 152: Can you spot a Mickey hat?
2 points

★ Now scan the wall mural inside **Mickey's Star Traders** shop.

Clue 153: Look for the train on the mural.
2 points

Clue 154: Find the Hidden Stitch.
3 points

Clue 155: Spot Mickey hats on a building.
2 points

Clue 156: Look up higher at the satellite dishes.
2 points

Clue 157: Scan closely for the road formation.
3 points

Clue 158: Find three clear domes.
2 points

Clue 159: Follow the mural around to another classic Mickey on a building.
1 point

★ Walk over to the **Tomorrowland Video Arcade** at the exit of *Space Mountain*.

Clue 160: Search around inside the arcade for classic Mickeys.
2 points

★ Cross the nearest bridge to **Main Street, U.S.A.** and search for 15 classic Mickeys as you stroll toward the park entrance.

Clue 161: Look around the outside of The Crystal Palace restaurant.
3 points

Clue 162: Check out a classic Mickey image in the Main Street Bakery.
3 points

Clue 163: Inside the Emporium store, study the merchandise stands.
2 points

Clue 164: Near the Emporium store outside, search for Hidden Mickeys on a sign.
3 points

Clue 165: Observe the overhead moving candy bins in the Main Street Confectionery near Town Square.
3 points

Clue 166: Closely examine the Caffe Italiano coffee cart (present seasonally) near Tony's Town Square Restaurant.
2 points

Clue 167: Study the floor inside Tony's Town Square Restaurant for a classic Mickey.
5 points

Clue 168: Now look around inside the restaurant for a classic Mickey under a painting.
3 points

Clue 169: Search for a classic Mickey in a

display cabinet inside Town Square Exposition Hall.
3 points

Clue 170: Inside Town Square Exposition Hall, look for a Hidden Mickey on each of two dogs.
4 points for spotting both

Clue 171: Also inside Exposition Hall, spot a classic Mickey on a bush.
3 points

Clue 172: Find Hidden Mickeys on Main Street's horse-drawn trolley.
2 points

Clue 173: Look around the Main Street Train Station for a Hidden Mickey on a ticket.
4 points

Clue 174: Find a Hidden Mickey on the wall inside the Main Street Train Station.
3 points

★ End your scavenger hunt by riding the **WDW Railroad** around the park to search out another Hidden Mickey.

Clue 175: Try to spot the reclining Mickey in the clouds as your train chugs through *Splash Mountain*.
4 points

★ Enjoy the **SpectroMagic parade** in the evening and be on the lookout for Hidden Mickeys!

Clue 176: Stare in front of Mickey Mouse for a classic Mickey.
3 points

Clue 177: Search near *Aladdin*'s Genie for a classic Mickey.
4 points

(Tip: You can often spot a classic Mickey in the sky during the evening *Wishes* fireworks show. If you see one, give yourself 5 extra points!)

★ If you go through the **Transportation and Ticket Center**, check out a cool Hidden Mickey.

Clue 178: Study the ceiling skylights.
5 points

Total Points for Magic Kingdom =

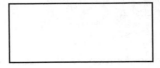

How'd you do?
Up to 227 points – Bronze
228 – 456 points – Silver
457 points and over – Gold
571 points - Perfect Score

(If you earned bonus points in the *Judge's Tent*, you may have done even better!)

**Caution:
Don't peek at this
section unless you
really want help!**

Main Street, U.S.A.

- Train Station

Hint 1: The periphery of the Main Street Train Station roof, second level, has scrollwork that repeats a classic Mickey motif.

Frontierland

- Big Thunder Mountain Railroad

Hint 2: Three stalagmites in the cavern to your right at the beginning of the ride form a classic Mickey. Look down at the left side of the floor of the cavern.

Hint 3: At the end of the ride, just past the dinosaur bones on the right side of the track, you'll see sets of gear wheels lying on the ground. The second set of gears resembles a classic Hidden Mickey. (The dimensions aren't quite classic, but this is a sentimental favorite.)

Hint 4: On the left side as you exit the ride, a cutout in the reddish rock resembles a side profile of Tinker Bell. She's behind the fence, behind a cactus and between two metal carts. (It's the exit closest to the standby line entrance.)

- *Splash Mountain*

Hint 5: A red classic Hidden Mickey is painted on a yoke that hangs on a left wall of the entrance queue. It's in the first tunnel. Start looking for it when you reach the part of the tunnel with lights on the wall. You can spot it from both the standby and FASTPASS queues.

Hint 6: During the first part of the ride, when your boat is outside, look to your right for a barrel with "Muskrat Moonshine" painted on the side. A classic Mickey is formed by holes in the paint, above the "s" in "Muskrat."

Hint 7: Halfway up the second crankhill, on the right side, three barrels in the lower right corner of a stack of barrels form a classic Mickey.

Hint 8: Look for a picnic basket up on a small ledge. You'll spot it just past Brer Frog, who is sitting on an alligator and fishing with his toe. Near the basket are three red-and-white-striped fishing bobbers in the shape of a classic Hidden Mickey.

Hint 9: On the right side of your boat, in the room with jumping water, a classic rope Mickey is hanging half-way down from the ceiling. It's in the shadows behind a lantern and just past the turtle lying on a geyser.

Hint 10: The hole in the mountain at the top of the big drop is sculpted to form a side profile of Mickey's face. As you approach the big drop in your boat, Mickey's nose juts out from the left side of the hole. (You can also see this one from the outside viewing area; see Hint 14.)

Hint 11: Near the end of the ride, the upper outline of one of the white clouds on the right side of the riverboat scene is shaped

like Mickey Mouse lying on his back, with his head to the right. (This Hidden Mickey is also visible from the *Walt Disney World Railroad* train as it passes through *Splash Mountain*; see Clue and Hint 175.)

Hint 12: A birdhouse with a rope ladder in the entrance queue (also visible as you exit) has a classic Mickey acorn formation above a door and below blue roof slats. Another classic Mickey made of acorns is near the peanut shell chimney, above the curve of the red rail. You'll find it the birdhouse just past the photo viewing area.

Hint 13: Inside the huge "log" that parallels *Splash Mountain*'s exit walkway and is part of the "Laughin' Place" children's play area, an upside down classic Mickey can be found on the end of a small log that appears to be about to break through the inner wall of the huge log. Tall adults will have to bend over to walk inside the big log to see it.

Hint 14: Walk in front of *Splash Mountain* after your ride. The hole in the mountain for the big drop forms a side profile of Mickey's face. From the outside, Mickey's nose juts out from the right side of the hole.

Adventureland

- Pirates of the Caribbean

Hint 15: Along the left entrance queue is a room with a faux fireplace on the right side. A classic Mickey is in the plaster on the sloping area to the right and above the fireplace mantle. It's about seven feet up from the floor.

Hint 16: Tall gun cabinets stand on both sides of the left entrance queue. On two of the cabinets are classic-Mickey-shaped locks (one on each side).

Hint 17: About halfway along the left queue, a pile of cannonballs appears on the floor to your left. A classic Mickey made of cannonballs is on the lower left area of the pile.

Hint 18: At the beginning of the ride, Davy Jones's image is projected on a wall of mist in front of the boat. Look up at the left side of his hat (his right side, viewers' left). Below and to the left of the bottom of the "V" at the front of his hat, three tiny gold balls form a classic Mickey.

Hint 19: About halfway through the ride and past the red-haired lady, a cat behind an intoxicated pirate casts a classic Hidden Mickey moving shadow on the corner of the wall above and behind it.

Hint 20: We float under this pirate on the bridge, who sits over us with his leg hanging down. On the pirate's hat, the skull's left eye (on our right) looks like a classic Mickey.

Hint 21: As your boat approaches the last scene (the treasure room), a classic Mickey lock hangs on large wooden recessed doors to the left.

Hint 22: Classic Mickey metal loops are at the bottom of several of the lanterns in the last scene. Stare at the closest lantern on a post to the left of your boat. As the background lighting changes, the tiny classic Mickey hanging at the bottom of this lantern will come into view.

Hint 23: As the treasure room comes into view, a classic Mickey lock hangs at the middle of the wooden door that's swung open on the left. A long key juts out of the keyhole of the lock.

Hint 24: Classic Mickey locks hang on the cabinets behind Captain Jack Sparrow in the treasure room.

Hint 25: Just as you enter the gift shop after exiting your boat, several classic Mickeys are formed by coins and jewels in hanging plates near the right wall. Look along the edges of the plates for some of the best images.

Hint 26: Rocks forming a classic Mickey are in "The Crow's Nest" shop, inside and on the right of the front display case. This shop is at the edge of Adventureland, near Frontierland.

Frontierland

- Frontierland Shootin' Arcade

Hint 27: In the front center of the target area is a group of cactus plants. One near the middle has three lobes forming a classic Hidden Mickey.

Liberty Square

- Stocks near the Liberty Square Riverboat entrance

Hint 28: Padlocks on the stocks near the entrance are shaped to resemble classic Hidden Mickeys (even though the "ears" are a bit small).

- The Haunted Mansion

Hint 29: Just inside the entrance to the first room, you'll find some small classic Mickeys in the oval border design around the portrait of the dressed-up aging man above the fireplace.

Hint 30: As you pass by the library room (at the beginning of the ride) and then the "endless hallway" on your right, check out the backs of two purple chairs for an abstract Donald Duck. Near the top of the chairs, you can see his cap, which sits above his distorted eyes, face, and bill. (Note that the chair may change locations at times.)

Hint 31: A plate and two saucers on the ghostly banquet table are arranged to form a classic Mickey. They're usually at the bottom left corner of the table.

Hint 32: In the first part of the attic area, on the floor to your left under a small table with shelves, plates form a classic Mickey.

Hint 33: To the right of the opera singing lady (her left) is a ghost resembling the grim reaper. He is holding up his left arm. Hanging from his left hand is a cloth with markings at the top that form a classic Hidden Mickey.

49

Hint 34: Stand slightly to the left and under the last chandelier along the exit hallway. Two lights on the left side shine on the ceiling and form the "ears" for the circular chandelier's "head."

Hint 35: Outside, at the left end of the covered walkway, a classic Mickey metal latch holds a wrought iron gate open.

Hint 36: In the pet cemetery on the left side of the outside exit walkway, a Mr. Toad tombstone stands at the rear left corner.

- Columbia Harbour House restaurant

Hint 37: In the downstairs table area, a wall across from the food-order counters is decorated with three small circular maps covered by a single piece of glass. (The central map is labeled "Charles V.") The three circles form a classic Mickey.

Tomorrowland

- near Tomorrowland Indy Speedway

Hint 38: A tall lamp post casts a classic Mickey shadow on the pavement. It's best seen on a sunny day during the late morning or early afternoon.

Mickey's Toontown Fair

Hint 39: On the streets, look for classic Hidden Mickeys on the upper edges of the merchandise carts.

- approaching and in Minnie's Country House

Hint 40: The front of the chimney outdoors includes three stones that form a classic Mickey. They are just left of where the roof and chimney meet.

Hint 41: In the first room, wallpaper along the upper border of the wall has classic Mickeys made of yellow and pink flowers.

Hint 42: In the second room, a side-profile Hidden Mickey can be seen near the bottom of the spine of the left-most book (entitled "My Fair Mouse"). The book is on the second shelf of a bookshelf on the right wall.

Hint 43: Along the right wall of the second room, tiny classic Mickeys are on the bottom right of a portrait of Clarabelle Cow.

Hint 44: In Minnie's sewing room, a large quilt on the wall has yellow classic Mickey heads on every other square and a blue classic Mickey in the center of the blue ribbon. Other blue-ribbon classic Mickeys are hanging around the room.

Hint 45: A tall orange pot on a shelf near the door has Mickey ears.

Hint 46: Minnie Mouse is in a picture (one of the "Minnie's Cartoon Country Living" magazine covers) in the hallway to her kitchen. Mickey ears sit on the top of her mirror.

Hint 47: Red Barns is in a picture (one of the "Minnie's Cartoon Country Living" magazine covers) in the hallway to Minnie's kitchen. His string tie clasp is a classic Mickey.

Hint 48: Before Minnie's kitchen, in a display window on your left, a small ceramic Mickey house has classic Mickey-shaped pumpkins out back and classic Mickey-shaped windows in the rear door.

Hint 49: On a table just inside Minnie's kitchen, a plate and two teacups are arranged as a classic Mickey.

Hint 50: Over the stove in Minnie's kitchen, a frying pan and two pots form a classic Mickey head.

Hint 51: Inside the refrigerator, a bottle of cheese relish in the door has a red classic Mickey "brand mark" at the top of the label.

Hint 52: Salt and pepper shakers with classic Mickey tops are in an upper cabinet at the rear left of Minnie's kitchen.

- approaching and in Mickey's Country House

Hint 53: As you head into the house, look for classic Mickeys:
- on the mailbox in front.
- on top of the front fence.
- above the front bay window.
- on the front door.

Hint 54: Look along the edge of the rug in Mickey's bedroom for more classic Mickeys.

Hint 55: Across from the front door is a set of keys hanging on the wall. One end of a black key is shaped like a classic Mickey. The mirror on the wall above the keys also looks like Mickey.

Hint 56: A white envelope with a Mickey stamp is on a table across from the front door entrance.

Hint 57: The design inside the blue fence includes classic Mickey holes as well as décor Mickeys on top of the fence.

Hint 58: In Mickey's living room on the coffee table, there is a noisemaker with a classic Mickey made of a yellow head and orange ears. The table is in front of the couch, on the right side of the room.

Hint 59: In the game room, first check the shape of the checkers on the checkerboard. Then look closely at the ping-pong paddles: one is shaped like Mickey's head and the other like Donald's. A paddle with Goofy's hat is on a lower shelf above some books, at the rear left of the game room across from the kitchen.

Hint 60: On the right side of the white tarp draped over the refrigerator in Mickey's kitchen, a green paint splotch is shaped like a side-profile Mickey image.

Hint 61: On the upper border of the wallpaper near the ceiling, on the right side of the kitchen, is a classic Mickey formed from an orange and two limes.

Hint 62: The paint cans in the sink of Mickey's kitchen have Mickey on the labels.

Hint 63: Just inside the second window of the kitchen, the scale in the bottom right-hand corner of the renovation blueprints includes a distorted classic Mickey: the third image from the left. Another small (undistorted) classic Mickey image is repeated in the middle of the blueprints, to the right of the yellow writing pad.

Hint 64: The design and contents of Mickey's backyard change periodically, but here are a few classic Mickeys you are likely to see:
- the hedge and grass garden together form Mickey's head. The grass is the head and the hedge forms his ears.
- tomato Mickeys.
- pumpkin Mickeys.

Hint 65: A classic Mickey made of rocks can usually be found on the ground to the left of the backyard path, past Pluto's doghouse and before the large pumpkins. The rocks change position occasionally and are sometimes inside the pink pot with the artificial plants.

Hint 66: A classic Mickey is low down on the back of a pole that has a sign pointing to the Judge's Tent.

Hint 67: The handle on the water fixture in the backyard garden is a three-circle Hidden Mickey. It's to the right of the back door of the house.

Hint 68: In Mickey's garage, three hubcaps on the upper back wall form a classic Hidden Mickey, and the front middle window of a birdhouse on a table is also shaped like a classic Mickey.

- in the Judge's Tent

The interior arrangements of this attraction change frequently, so I don't know what Hidden Mickeys you may find when you visit. You can count on seeing a number of décor Mickeys if you decide to wait long enough to meet Mickey (and it will be a wait!). Just keep your eyes open. In the Main Mouse's room, examine the walls closely for a classic Mickey in the centers of blue ribbons decorating the walls and give yourself an extra bonus point. Add another bonus point for spotting the classic Mickey along the top rail of a small desk at the right wall.

- Donald's Boat

Hint 69: Donald and Daisy are on a wall map inside *Donald's Boat*. A peninsula on the right side is shaped like Donald. A bay at the top center forms Daisy, and she's holding a daisy!

- The Barnstormer at Goofy's Wiseacre Farm

Hint 70: Along the entrance queue, a weather vane outside (above the silo on the right) looks like Mickey's side profile.

Hint 71: Inside the first barn of the entrance queue, some small blue classic Mickeys are painted on the top of a helicopter, which is hanging from the ceiling in the second display area to the left of the queue.

Hint 72: Along the right side of the entrance queue, after you pass through the barn, the fifth (or so) mounted fan has a classic Mickey in the decorative ironwork inside its support.

Hint 73: On the sign for the Wacky Radio shack to the right of *The Barnstormer* ride, the knot in the necktie worn by the rooster DJ is a classic Mickey.

Hint 74: On the left, inside the County Bounty Store, a large cowboy hat atop a merchandise stand has a classic Mickey decal.

Tomorrowland

Hint 75: On the right side of the display at the top of the FASTPASS machines for *Buzz Lightyear's Space Ranger Spin* is a classic Mickey with red ears.

- Monsters, Inc. Laugh Floor

Hint 76: On the outside wall, a picture advertising a Recreational Rocket has a moon with craters shaped like an upside-down classic Mickey.

Hint 77: Also on the outside wall, a sign advertising a Space Collectibles Convention includes an asteroid shaped like a classic Mickey head.

Hint 78: As you enter the attraction, look for a window display of a city on the rear of the right-hand wall just past the entrance doors to the second room. A classic Mickey is under the apex of the triangular roof segment on the building in the front center of the window display.

- Walt Disney's Carousel of Progress

Hint 79: In the third scene, Mickey's Sorcerer's Hat sits at the right side of the room, next to the girl in the shaker machine.

Hint 80: In the last scene, an abstract Mickey Mouse as the Sorcerer's apprentice from *Fantasia* is in a painting on the dining room wall. To spot it, look immediately to the left rear of the scene as it rotates into view. The painting is on the dining room's right rear wall.

Hint 81: On the left side of the room, a nutcracker shaped like Mickey Mouse stands on the left side of the mantelpiece.

Hint 82: Under the Christmas tree is a box with a plush Mickey Mouse.

Hint 83: On the last stage, one of the Christmas presents under the tree (near the grandfather's chair) has a large classic Mickey head cut out of green paper glued to the side of the gift. The gift is partially hidden by another present, so you see the ears and part of the top of Mickey's head. The green Mickey ears are to the right of Grandpa's lower leg and behind the present with the silver bow.

Hint 84: A classic Mickey appears (just for a few seconds) on the top of a spaceship in the middle of the television screen. Look for it just as the game starts on the TV, before Grandma starts playing.

Hint 85: A pepper grinder on the kitchen counter has Mickey ears. Look for it as you exit the room.

Hint 86: Along the exit ramps, classic Mickeys are on the backs of the round signs for the attraction.

- Buzz Lightyear's Space Ranger Spin

Hint 87: Just inside the building, in the entrance queue, the second poster on the right wall is called "Planets of the Galactic Alliance." In Sector 1, the central continent on the planet "Pollost Prime" is shaped like a profile of Mickey Mouse's head in outline.

Hint 88: This same planet appears in the top left of a recessed wall further along the entrance queue, to the left of the large View Master.

Hint 89: Sector 2 in this same mural contains a planet made of many spheres, some of which form classic Mickeys. One of them is at the outer edge of the planet at about the "10 o'clock" location.

Hint 90: You go through three different rooms during the first part of this ride. When you enter the room with lots of batteries, look to the left of the ride vehicle. You'll see a side profile of Mickey's head in the rear left under the words, "Initiate Battery Unload."

Hint 91: As the ride vehicle moves through the space video room, planet "Pollost Prime," with continent Mickey, flies by on the right wall.

Hint 92: Just past the space video room, in the final battle scene on the ride, "Pollost Prime" shows up yet again on a wall straight ahead and to the upper left.

Hint 93: A yellow classic Mickey is on the wall across from the video monitors that show ride photos. An alien is pointing up to it.

Hint 94: Stitch's spaceship is flying through

space in a corner of the first mural on the right wall as you exit the ride.

Hint 95: Just before you see Zurg behind bars, a star field on your right includes two classic Mickeys, one at the lower right and another smaller one at the top center.

- Astro Orbiter

Hint 96: A small classic Mickey is traced in the cement close to a support beam near *Astro Orbiter* on the side toward *Space Mountain*, between Cool Ship and The Lunching Pad.

Liberty Square

- The Hall of Presidents

Hint 97: On a wall painting in the waiting room for the show, a tiny classic Mickey is at the end of the object George Washington holds in his left hand.

- Liberty Square Riverboat

Hint 98: At the right end of the bridge from Frontierland (as you face it from the boat), three rocks form a classic Mickey. They're located between the last two vertical posts that support the handrail, about one foot down from the top of the rocks. (Note: This Hidden Mickey is also visible from *Tom Sawyer Island*.)

- afternoon parade

Hint 99: Classic Mickeys are in the confetti decorations on the "Celebrate" banner that's carried at the front of the afternoon parade, and the Grand Marshal's vehicle is covered with them. The vehicle, which carries the family selected to be that day's Grand Marshals, has classic Mickeys on its tire treads, front bumper, and hood ornament, as well as on the nuts at the side of the front windshield, the tread on the spare tire on the rear of the car, the brackets holding the spare tire in place, and even the confetti images on the outside of the car.

Hint 100: Classic Mickeys hide in the confetti decorations along the sides of Mickey's parade float.

Hint 101: On Pinocchio's float, you will find a classic Mickey imprint on a wooden panel in front of the Dwarf playing the piano on the left side of the float. A statue of Walt Disney and Mickey stands on a shelf behind a clock on the right side of the float. An etched glass image of Walt Disney walking in Disneyland may be seen on the lower back part of the float with the castle spires.

Hint 102: Classic Mickeys are in the confetti decorations on the final parade banner.

(Note: Hidden Character images on parade floats may come and go or change location over time.)

- Tom Sawyer Island

Hint 103: Halfway through Old Scratch's Mystery Mine, bright shining gems embedded in the wall form a side profile of Goofy. He's looking to your right.

Fantasyland

- Snow White's Scary Adventures

Hint 104: The loading area mural shows the Dwarves' laundry hanging on a line. On the left side of a pair of boxer shorts (the third pair from the right) is a red classic Mickey.

Hint 105: Below the bird and two flowers on the chimney in the loading area mural, three gray stones form a classic Mickey.

Hint 106: In the first part of the ride, the mirror that the Wicked Queen is looking into has three circles on top that form a classic Mickey.

Hint 107: Early in the ride, look for the green turtle climbing stairs to the left of your ride vehicle. The large circle on the left side of its shell forms the "head" of a classic Mickey.

Hint 108: Later in the ride, when you see the sign for the Dwarves' Mine, look closely to the right as your car curves to enter the mine. On the lower part of the right entrance panel, you'll see a drawing of Mickey (with a big nose) dressed as a Dwarf and carrying a shovel.

- Peter Pan's Flight

Hint 109: At the lower right of the entrance sign cloud formation is an incomplete classic cloud Mickey. All you can see is the top of the head and the ears. It's just to the right of the "t" in "Peter," and Peter Pan is standing between Mickey's ears.

Hint 110: Close to the entrance turnstile, a group of trees faces the loading area. The fourth tree from the far end has a dark classic Mickey in the bark about halfway up the trunk.

Hint 111: At the beginning of the ride, as your ship flies into the children's bedroom, three cookies on a plate in the middle of a table to your right form a classic Mickey.

Hint 112: Three brown rocks in the yard in front of the doghouse form a classic Mickey. The rocks are in the brown dirt section of the yard. Mickey's smiling face may be on the "head" rock, but it's hard to spot!

Hint 113: On the rocky edge of the mermaid lagoon, three flowers on the grass form a classic Mickey; the "head" is yellow and the "ears" are light orange.

- The Many Adventures of Winnie the Pooh

Hint 114: At the beginning of the ride, in Rabbit's Garden, the small marker with radishes (in the middle pot to the left of the "Letus" sign) has one radish shaped like a classic Hidden Mickey.

Hint 115: At the beginning of the left wall of Owl's house (the second room on the ride)

is a picture of Mr. Toad handing the deed to the house over to Owl (a tribute to the previous attraction in this building, *Mr. Toad's Wild Ride*).

Hint 116: Near the end of this room, on the right side of the floor, is a picture of Mole standing with Winnie the Pooh.

- Mickey's PhilharMagic

Hint 117: In the first waiting area inside, the wall mural with musical instruments has several small white classic Mickeys.

Hint 118: On the right vertical border of the video screen in the main theater, a classic Mickey hides inside a French horn.

Hint 119: In the "Be Our Guest" portion of the movie, there is a point where you are watching Lumiere dancing on the table with other characters. The view goes to an overhead shot and there are shadows cast on the table from the candle hands of Lumiere. These shadows come together at times to form what appears to be a Hidden Mickey.

Hint 120: In "The Little Mermaid" segment, Ariel throws out jewels in the water in front of her. Stay focused on the right side of the screen (your right), to spot a ring as it rotates slowly from a rim position to an open circle. A dark classic Mickey image is visible just as you first spot the open center of the ring. The image disappears as the ring finishes its rotation.

Hint 121: Watch closely as Aladdin and Jasmine ride their magic carpet in the sky. Stare at the bottom left of the screen for a quick glimpse of three round buildings on the ground, clustered to form a classic Mickey.

Hint 122: Some circles in the carpet along the exit walkway form classic Mickeys.

Hint 123: Music stands shaped like classic Mickeys are on shelves high up above the merchandise in Fantasy Faire Shop at the exit of *Mickey's PhilharMagic*.

- Pinocchio Village Haus restaurant

Hint 124: As you head from the dining area to the restrooms, a tiny dark classic Mickey appears above the word "dreams" on the left wall near the exit to the restrooms.

Hint 125: On the left side of this "When you wish upon a star" mural (near the exit to the restrooms), a tiny white classic Mickey is near a sparkling star. It's to the left of the Fairy, at the level of her mid right thigh, and her right thumb points to it.

- Fairytale Garden

Hint 126: At the base of the first light pole on the right as you enter, a classic Mickey that looks like a piece of different colored stucco is in the cement on the side next to the fence.

Hint 127: A side profile of Pluto's head is on the wall, upper left of the stage. It's left of the brick circle and above the stairs.

- "it's a small world"

Hint 128: Toward the end of the Africa room, vines on the right above the giraffes and to the left of your boat have purple leaves shaped like classic Mickey heads.

Hint 129: In the South America room, a pumpkin and two pineapples on the floor to the right of the boat form a classic Mickey.

Hint 130: Near the end of the South Pacific room, several koala bears hang on a tree. As you approach the bears on your left, the back of the blue bear's head forms a classic Mickey.

- near Peter Pan's Flight

Hint 131: Between Peter Pan's Flight and the restrooms nearby, next to Liberty Square, you'll find paintings of grape clusters on the walls.

The lower three grapes in the second cluster from the right at the bottom form a classic Mickey.

- Pooh's Playful Spot

Hint 132: Inside the big tree, a classic Mickey is formed by embedded rocks above the frame of the smaller children's entrance.

Hint 133: Above the frame of the larger entrance inside the big tree is a depression in the wood shaped like a submarine: a tribute to the previous *20,000 Leagues Under the Sea* attraction at this location; thus, a hidden tribute rather than a Hidden Mickey.

Hint 134: On the outside of the big tree, in back, a side profile of Mickey is carved into the bark. It's at the upper left corner above the lower window.

- Sir Mickey's Store

Hint 135: You'll find a classic Mickey toward the top of the store's sign-shield. The shield is hanging under a vine, across from Tinker Bell's Treasures shop.

Liberty Square

- Outside The Yankee Trader shop

Hint 136: A classic Mickey with hoofprints for ears and a water utility cover for a head can be found in the cement equidistant between The Yankee Trader shop and the Columbia Harbour House restaurant, near the red cement.

Hint 137: A tiny red classic Mickey is painted on a finger on the side of Madame Leota's shopping stand.

- Ye Olde Christmas Shoppe

Hint 138: Inside the shop, a classic Hidden Mickey is formed by three logs in the upper left corner of a stack of logs in the framed log collage under a register in the middle of the store.

Frontierland

- Frontier Trading Post store

Hint 139: A "How to Pin Trade" sign, behind a register inside the store to the right, sports a rope classic Mickey. Another rope classic Mickey is above the merchandise, facing the middle entrance to the store.

Hint 140: In the "How to Pin Trade" posters, a cowboy's lanyard has a black classic Mickey.

Adventureland

- The Enchanted Tiki Room – Under New Management

Hint 141: Upside-down classic Mickeys are camouflaged in the designs at the bottom of two bird perches. One perch is in the left corner as you enter the theater. The other is to the right of the exit door.

Hint 142: To the right of the entrance to *The Enchanted Tiki Room*, a statue with several faces has classic Mickeys formed by beads in the middle of the forehead, above the nose.

- near the Magic Carpets of Aladdin

Hint 143: A charm embedded in the cement between the *Magic Carpets of Aladdin* exit and the Agrabah Bazaar shop contains a tiny classic Mickey. It's near a shop pole that has a strip of purple paint at the top of its base.

- Jungle Cruise

Hint 144: Along the right side of the boat, watch for the Pygmy War Canoes sitting on a beach. The bow of the middle canoe resembles Donald Duck.

Hint 145: After the waterfall, a wrecked silver plane sits to the right of the boat. Look back to spot three circles etched in the metal at the lower right of the visible section of fuselage. The circles are all the same size, but many folks and Cast Members consider them a Hidden Mickey.

Hint 146: Along the left side of the boat, be alert for menacing natives with spears. The last isolated native of the group wears a Donald mask.

Hint 147: The first undecorated column on the left wall (the third column from the end as you come out of the temple) has a chipped area of brick on the third block from the top. The chipped area forms part of a profile view of Mickey's head and face. Don't get discouraged if you have trouble spotting it; this one is tough to find — especially the first time.

- Swiss Family Treehouse

Hint 148: A side profile of Mickey, facing to the right, is on a section of the tree trunk that touches a wall of the treehouse. Mickey is in a clearing inside a large patch of green algae, on the right as you descend the steps from the boys' bedroom and on the left as you walk down from the very top of the trail.

Hint 149: In the open dining area at the bottom of the walking trail, a plate and two cups form a classic Mickey. It's usually at the lower right end of the dinner table.

Tomorrowland

- Tomorrowland Transit Authority

Hint 150: The woman getting her hair done sports a belt buckle with a classic Hidden Mickey.

- Merchant of Venus shop

Hint 151: Face the cash registers and look at the mural on the wall behind the left side register. In the foreground is one of Stitch's cousins holding a Mickey balloon.

Hint 152: In the same mural, another cousin of Stitch is wearing Mickey ears.

- Mickey's Star Traders shop

Hint 153: On the wall mural, the headlights of a train form a classic Mickey.

Hint 154: Stitch races beside a train in the mural.

Hint 155: Mickey hats sit atop windows halfway up the sides of a building.

Hint 156: Satellite dishes form a classic Mickey on top of this building.

Hint 157: Across the room on another wall mural, the middle circle of freeway loops forms a classic Mickey.

Hint 158: Over one of the entrance doors, clear domes form a classic Mickey.

Hint 159: The blue glass dome covering one building is a classic Mickey with ears.

Hint 160: Inside the Tomorrowland Video Arcade, classic Mickey images repeat in the background of the curtains covering the front of the photo booths in the Portrait Studio area.

Main Street, U.S.A.

Hint 161: On the roof of The Crystal Palace restaurant, the circles in the middle row of the tower above the main entrance resemble Mickey ears.

Hint 162: Along the left side of the Main Street Bakery entrance queue, a Mickey-shaped serving platter is partially hidden in the upper left of a display case. Other plate arrangements in the display cabinet aren't proportioned properly to be Hidden Mickeys.

Hint 163: In the Emporium store, metal poles that hold up merchandise shelves sport classic Mickey holes.

Hint 164: Outside along Main Street, just to

the right of the Emporium shop and near the Athletic Club, a sign on a door has two classic Mickeys at the top and bottom along the border.

Hint 165: Candy bins in the Main Street Confectionery move along a track suspended from the ceiling. On the lower front and back sides of the bins are holes arranged like classic Mickeys.

Hint 166: The sign on the Caffe Italiano cart, which appears seasonally in front of Tony's Town Square Restaurant, includes a classic Mickey in its design.

Hint 167: When you enter the inside dining area of Tony's Town Square Restaurant, look immediately to your right to the bureau against the wall. A classic Mickey image is on the first complete (not partially covered) black square floor tile in the middle front of the bureau, at the right lower corner of the tile as you face the bureau.

Hint 168: A classic Mickey made of bread rolls is to the right as you enter the dining area inside Tony's Town Square Restaurant. It's sitting on an armoire under a painting from *Lady and the Tramp*.

Hint 169: A camera in a display cabinet on the right side of the left hallway inside Town Square Exposition Hall sports a classic Mickey.

Hint 170: In the rear theater of Town Square Exposition Hall, each of two young Dalmatians in one of the photo prop scenes bears a black classic Mickey spot.

Hint 171: In another photo prop scene in the same theater, a bush in the lower middle of a backdrop mural (behind Mickey Mouse in a boat) is shaped like a classic Mickey. It's at the bottom right side of a group of bushes.

Hint 172: Several classic Mickeys adorn the gear of the horse pulling the Main Street Trolley.

Hint 173: At the Main Street Train Station's faux ticket office upstairs, an image that looks like Mickey is on a baggage ticket next to the letter "K" inside the front window to the right. (Walk up the outside stairs to the office window, which faces Main Street.)

Hint 174: A classic Mickey-shaped lock can also be found inside the faux ticket office. Look for the lock hanging on the right wall behind the windows.

- from the WDW Railroad

Hint 175: In the riverboat scene near the end of the *Splash Mountain* ride, the upper outline of one of the white clouds on the right is shaped like Mickey Mouse lying on his back, his head to the right.

Note: This Hidden Mickey is also visible from the *Splash Mountain* ride (see Clue and Hint 11).

- SpectroMagic parade

Hint 176: Watch Mickey's float. A classic Mickey is inside the glass globe in front of Mickey Mouse.

Hint 177: Look in front of Genie for a small, white classic Mickey on his music stand.

Transportation and Ticket Center

Hint 178: An imprint of Mickey's face, full frontal image, has remained over the years. It looks as though it was made by a balloon that melted against the glass. This Hidden Mickey is in the second overhead glass bubble from the tram, in the first row of bubble skylights to the right as you walk from the trams toward the monorail entrance ramps.

Notes

Epcot
Scavenger Hunt

• •

If you arrive early in the day, as I recommend, ask if *Soarin'*, *Test Track*, and *Mission: SPACE* — the attractions in which I start the Epcot Scavenger Hunt — are open now. If not, do the *Living with the Land* ride (Clues 88 to 95) first and come back to *Soarin'*, *Test Track*, and *Mission: SPACE*.

Note: Many of the Hidden Mickeys in this park are in restaurants and shops. Be considerate of fellow guests and Cast Members as you search. Tell them what you're looking for, so they can share in the fun. Avoid searching restaurants at busy meal times unless you are one of the diners.

★ Walk briskly to **Soarin'** in The Land Pavilion.

Clue 1: Along the entrance queue, five screens show changing artistic landscapes. Search for Mickey in the landscape with the purple mountain ridge in the lower background.
4 points

Clue 2: In the pre-show video, spot the Mickey ears.
2 points

Clue 3: In the pre-show video, stay alert for Hidden Character clothing logos.
4 points for spotting both

Clue 4: While soaring, look left for a Mickey balloon.
4 points

Clue 5: Then look right for a Mickey shadow.
4 points

Clue 6: Don't blink at the golf ball!
5 points

Clue 7: A huge classic Mickey in the sky

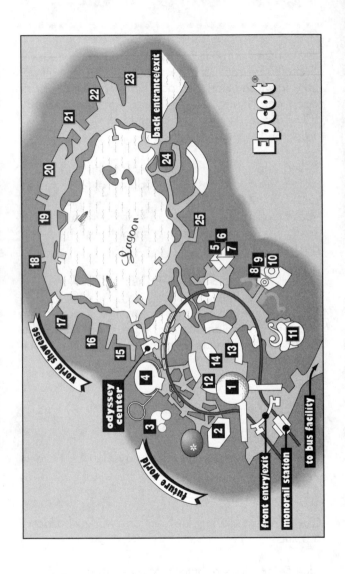

Epcot®

FUTURE WORLD

1. Spaceship Earth Pavilion
2. Universe of Energy Pavilion
3. Mission: SPACE Pavilion
4. Test Track Pavilion

Imagination! Pavilion
5. Honey, I Shrunk the Audience
6. Journey Into Imagination with Figment
7. ImageWorks

The Land Pavilion
8. Living with the Land
9. The Circle of Life
10. Soarin'

11. The Seas with Nemo & Friends Pavilion
12. Innoventions East Side
13. Innoventions West Side
14. Innoventions Plaza

WORLD SHOWCASE

15. Mexico: Gran Fiesta Tour
16. Norway: Maelstrom
17. China: Reflections of China
18. Germany
19. Italy
20. The American Adventure: The American Adventure Show
21. Japan
22. Morocco
23. France: Impressions de France
24. United Kingdom
25. Canada: O Canada!

71

greets you at the end of your *Soarin'* ride.
3 points

★ Go to the walkway through Innoventions East Side and get a FASTPASS for *Test Track*. Start your hunt in the **Mission: SPACE** waiting queue. Three Hidden Mickeys wait to be found.

Clue 8: Along the entrance queue, search for a Hidden Mickey on a planet.
4 points

Clue 9: Spot a Hidden Mickey in "status lights" on a monitor.
4 points

Clue 10: Look for waveform images on a monitor that form a Hidden Mickey.
4 points

Clue 11: Just before launch, keep your eyes open for two identical Hidden Mickeys.
4 points

Clue 12: As you land on Mars, glance around for a Hidden Mickey on a building.
4 points

Clue 13: After the ride, look for a Hidden Mickey on a video console in the exhibit area.
2 points

Clue 14: Spot a Hidden Mickey on the ceiling of the gift shop at the attraction exit.
4 points

Clue 15: Search for Donald and Pluto on the ceiling.
4 points for spotting both

Clue 16: Squint for a small Hidden Mickey in a mural in the gift shop.
3 points

Clue 17: Look around for an upside-down classic Mickey in this mural.
3 points

Clue 18: Now glance low for classic Mickeys near the floor.
2 points

Clue 19: Find two classic Mickeys and a side-profile Mickey on the wall of the gift shop.
2 points for spotting all three

Clue 20: Outside in the front plaza, search for a classic Mickey on the moon.
3 points

Clue 21: Look down for a classic Mickey in the blue tile area out front.
5 points

Clue 22: In a blue tile stripe out front, spot a white classic Mickey near a black disk.
4 points

Clue 23: Find two more classic tile Mickeys near a drain cover.
4 points for spotting both

★ Go to **Test Track**.

Clue 24: Look for a Hidden Mickey among the objects on a tool chest.
3 points

Clue 25: Just before you get to the pre-show room, inspect the "Crash Test Vehicle" in area 5b carefully.
3 points

★ Find three more Mickeys near the knee calibration area. Psst!: The three are on the same desk exhibit.

Clue 26: Search out a classic Hidden Mickey.
2 points

Clue 27: Look higher for Mickey ears.
3 points

Clue 28: Then find a Mickey Mouse doll.
2 points

Clue 29: If you can manage to peek inside the first (single-riders queue) pre-show room, glance around for an orange Hidden Mickey on the wall.
3 points

Clue 30: Now look for another classic Mickey in the same room.
3 points

Clue 31: Keep alert for car S23 to spot a classic Mickey.
4 points

★ During the **Test Track ride**, try to find nine classic Mickeys. (Keep your eyes peeled; four of them are hard to spot.)

Clue 32: In the "Environmental Chambers," glance back for a classic Mickey above you to the right.
5 points

Clue 33: Look for the Mickey Mouse pencil in the first "Environmental Test" office.
2 points

Clue 34: In this same office, locate a classic Mickey made by a red Magic Marker.
3 points

Clue 35: Look to the left back wall of the cold room to find a classic Mickey.
5 points

Clue 36: Spot a Mickey Mouse doll in the second "Environmental Test" office.
3 points

★ In the "Corrosion Chamber" (the second chamber in the "Environmental Test" area), look fast to the right, then to the left to spot two classic Mickeys in rust.

Clue 37: On your right, check a hanging car door.
4 points

Clue 38: On your left, look for a truck fender.
4 points

Clue 39: After the "Environmental Chambers," stay alert for a white car on your right with a Mickey on its hood.
5 points

Clue 40: As you approach the crash barrier wall, try to spot the classic Mickey crash-test sticker on a white car to the left of your ride vehicle.
4 points

Clue 41: Then just before you reach the crash barrier wall, look at the floor to your left for one more.
4 points

Clue 42: After the ride, check out the monitors in the photo selection area for another look at the classic Mickey in Clue 41.
1 point

Possible bonus points: Also on the monitors, search for another classic Mickey behind the car. (Note: It's not always visible.)
3 points

Clue 43: Along the exit, spot Mickey on a sticker.
3 points

Clue 44: Then find Mickey on a name tag.
4 points

★ When World Showcase opens, take the path to the right of *Test Track*, heading toward World Showcase. Stop by the **Odyssey Center** building.

Clue 45: Glance inside for Mickey.
3 points

★ Go to **Maelstrom** in the Norway Pavilion. Study the loading area mural to find two Hidden Mickeys. Enjoy the ride and movie if you wish. (If there are Hidden Mickeys to be found in either, I haven't yet spotted them.)

Clue 46: Find the Viking wearing Mickey ears.
3 points

Clue 47: Look for the cruise director with Mickey's face outlined in the creases of her shirt. (This is a hard one to spot.)
4 points

Clue 48: Search for a Hidden Mickey inside the stave church outside.
4 points

★ Eat an early lunch to avoid the crowds. The San Angel Inn Restaurant is an ideal choice if you have 11:30 a.m. or so priority seating reservations. If not, try fast food at Cantina de San Angel at the Mexico Pavilion. Or try to get seated at Akershus Royal Banquet Hall in Norway (if you like seafood); it sometimes has tables available.

★ If you eat in the **San Angel Inn**, look for classic Mickeys in the smoke rising from the volcano (see Clue 41).

★ Go to **Gran Fiesta Tour Starring the Three Caballeros** in the Mexico Pavilion and keep your eyes peeled for classic Mickeys.

Clue 49: Find Mickey at the loading dock.
2 points

Clue 50: At the beginning of the ride, take a close look at the smoke rising from the volcano.
4 points

Clue 51: Spot classic Mickeys in a small blue pond to the left of the boat.
4 points

Clue 52: Don't miss Mickey in a barge!
3 points

★ After exiting the ride, walk to the **San Angel Inn restaurant** (if you haven't already been there) and look for classic Mickeys that appear and disappear.

Clue 53: Observe the smoke rising from the volcano. Ask the attendants to let you walk

to the fence by the river if you need a closer look.
4 points

★ Stroll over to **China**.

Clue 54: Search for Hidden Mickeys on posts in the courtyard.
4 points

Clue 55: Look around for Mickey outside near the theater.
3 points

★ Walk left to **Germany** to find four Hidden Mickeys.

Clue 56: As you walk into the plaza, look for the classic Mickey on a suit of armor on the building to your right.
3 points

Clue 57: Spot Mickey behind a large bell.
3 points

Clue 58: Can you find a Hidden Mickey in the landscaping of the exhibit?
3 points

★ Now check out the rest of the landscaping around the train attraction to earn some possible bonus points.
1 bonus point for each Hidden Mickey you spot.

(Note: These Hidden Mickeys come and go.)

★ Stop at **Italy** to inspect the shops.

Clue 59: Classic Mickeys are near the wine!
2 points

★ Go to **The American Adventure Pavilion** and inspect the rear wall of the rotunda, upstairs and down, for classic Hidden Mickeys.

Clue 60: Study a picture in the rotunda for Hidden Mickeys on two metal beams.
3 points for spotting both

77

Clue 61: Take a good look at the bronze eagle reliefs.
2 points for each floor; 4 points total

★ Now watch **The American Adventure show** and keep an eye out for three hard-to-spot classic Hidden Mickeys.

Clue 62: At the beginning of the film, look at the rocks behind a kneeling female pilgrim.
4 points

Clue 63: Stay alert for a Mickey image on a stockade.
3 points

Clue 64: At the end, watch the fireworks' explosions behind the Statue of Liberty Torch.
4 points

Clue 65: Outside, enjoy the **Fife and Drum Corps** and find four Hidden Mickeys. Check your Times Guide for performance times.
5 points for all spotting four

★ Stroll over to **Japan**.

Clue 66: Search for a classic Mickey in the koi fish pond.
2 points

Clue 67: Check out the grates at the base of the trees in the courtyard.
2 points

Clue 68: Look around for a bamboo Mickey near Yakitori House.
3 points

Clue 69: On your way to Morocco, don't miss the rock Mickey near the Mitsukoshi store!
5 points

★ Meander to **Morocco**.

Clue 70: Gaze at the exterior of the shop on the promenade.
2 points

Clue 71: Study a wall mural at the rear of the pavilion for three Hidden Mickeys.
5 points for spotting all three

★ Go to **France**.

Clue 72: Examine the grates at the base of the trees in the courtyard.
2 points

Clue 73: Find the classic Mickey bush on the right side of the ornamental garden.
3 points

Clue 74: Search for a Hidden Mickey on a book in a room near the shops.
5 points

Clue 75: Look high for classic Mickeys on the outside of a shop.
2 points

Clue 76: In the movie *Impressions de France*, spot Mickey's head and ears in the background of the wedding scene.
4 points

★ Enter the **United Kingdom**.

Clue 77: Check out a classic sports Mickey from the street.
2 points

★ Now walk over to **Canada** to find more classic Mickeys.

Clue 78: Examine the totem pole on the left near the steps into the pavilion.
3 points

Clue 79: Inside a store, search for Mickey on an animal.
4 points

Clue 80: Step inside Le Cellier Steakhouse for a Mickey made of wine.
3 points

★ Return to Future World and walk to Club Cool at the end of Innoventions West Side. Enjoy free exotic and refreshing soft drinks from foreign countries.

★ Get a FASTPASS for the *Living with the Land* ride in The Land Pavilion.

★ Head over to **The Seas with Nemo & Friends pavilion** to find nine Hidden Mickeys.

Clue 81: Look up along the entrance queue for the ride for a Hidden Mickey.
3 points

Clue 82: Keep alert on the ride for a Mickey in the rock. Look below the fifth video screen to spot it.
5 points

Clue 83: Walk upstairs and search for a Hidden Mickey on the Aquarium floor.
5 points

Clue 84: Downstairs, find two Hidden Mickeys in bubbles on the wall near the manatees.
5 points for spotting both

Clue 85: In Bruce's room downstairs, look around for classic Mickeys in two different windows.
4 points for spotting both

Clue 86: In the waiting area for "Turtle Talk with Crush," spot a tiny Mickey in the coral on the wall.
5 points

Clue 87: Search for Mickey near the exit gift shop.
3 points

★ Head right to the **Living with the Land** ride at your FASTPASS time. Study the wall murals to find three classic Hidden Mickeys.

Clue 88: Take a good look at the bubbles in the mural at the rear of the entrance queue.

80

3 points

Clue 89: Examine the mural behind the

loading area near the farmer's hat for Mickey.
3 points

Clue 90: Now check the lower part of the mural behind the loading area.
3 points

Clue 91: Keep alert for a Cast Member with a Hidden Mickey on a video screen.
4 points

Clue 92: Search for a garden hose classic Mickey. (This Hidden Mickey is also visible on the "Behind the Seeds" tour.)
4 points

Clue 93: Look for plants arranged as Hidden Mickeys. (These Hidden Mickeys may disappear at times.)
4 points

Clue 94: Toward the end of the ride, find the green Hidden Mickey in the round test tube holder in a lab room.
3 points

Clue 95: Stare at the planet Earth near the end of the ride for a cloud Mickey.
4 points

★ Go inside **The Garden Grill restaurant** upstairs and take a good look at the back wall.

Clue 96: Find and then marvel at the green face of Mickey Mouse on the left side of the large wall mural of vegetation. He's in three-quarter profile on the right side of a single fern and he's well camouflaged by the fern's leaves.
5 points

Clue 97: Observe Hidden Mickeys on the characters' clothing.
3 points

★ Go to the **railing to the left of the pavilion's main entrance**.

Clue 98: Focus on the side of one of the

globes hanging over the lobby to spot another Mickey.
3 points

Clue 99: As you face the entrance from outside, study the mosaic mural on the right wall for a classic Mickey in jewels.
4 points

Clue 100: If you take the "Behind the Seeds" tour, stay alert for a photo of the lettuce classic Mickey that you may have spotted earlier during the ride.
3 points

★ Keep your priority seating reservations for dinner. If you don't have reservations, eat at the Food Court in the Land Pavilion.

★ Go to the Imagination! Pavilion and ride **Journey Into Imagination with Figment**.

Clue 101: Squint for a black pair of Mickey ears in the Sight Room.
4 points

Clue 102: Look up at Figment's bathtub for a classic Mickey.
3 points

Clue 103: Now look up again in Figment's bathroom for another classic Mickey near the bathtub.
3 points

Clue 104: Find a classic Mickey on a cloud in the rainbow room.
3 points

Clue 105: Look for a classic Mickey on the wall along the exit hallway.
3 points

★ When you reach **ImageWorks** . . .

Clue 106: Search for a wall chart with a Hidden Mickey.
4 points

Clue 107: Then look down in *ImageWorks* for a classic Mickey.
4 points

★ Cross through Innoventions West Side and head for **Spaceship Earth**. Line up for the ride.

Clue 108: See if you can find the rocket with Mickey ears in its identification number. Psst! The rocket is in the mural.
2 points

Clue 109: During the ride, keep alert for classic Mickey light patterns on the floor to your right.
5 points

Clue 110: Watch to the left for a classic Mickey hiding among the scrolls on a shelf.
5 points

Clue 111: During the ride, notice the Hidden Mickey on the document in front of the sleeping monk.
4 points

Clue 112: In the Renaissance section, spot the classic Mickey formed by paint circles on a tabletop near a painter. Psst! Look quickly to your left.
4 points

Clue 113: Look for a chalkboard with the name of a famous Mickey Mouse cartoon.
4 points

Clue 114: As you enter the large computer room, find a Mickey image on your right. Psst! You can spot this image again in the large mirror on the rear wall as you pass by.
5 points for spotting both

Clue 115: Search for Mickey on a car.
4 points

Clue 116: After the car, Mickey appears on a wall.
4 points

Clue 117: After you exit the ride vehicle,

83

look up for Mickey in the "Project Tomorrow" area.
3 points

★ Cross back through the Innoventions buildings to the **Universe of Energy**. Find a Hidden Mickey as you take in the show and ride.

Clue 118: After the dinosaur section of the ride, watch the movie and look for the shadow of Disney's Hollywood Studios' "Earful" Tower (the tower with Mickey ears) in the door of a church in the background.
5 points

★ Walk to the **Tip Board** in Innoventions Plaza.

Clue 119: Look carefully at the continents on the rotating Earth that forms the "O" in Epcot.
4 points

★ Walk inside **Innoventions East**.

Clue 120: Spot a classic Mickey on the wall.
2 points

★ Go to the **Mouse Gear shop**, where you'll find a number of Hidden Mickeys and décor Mickeys.

Clue 121: Before you enter, find the classic Mickey in the sign above the shop entrance.
1 point

★ Now step inside, and keep your eyes peeled.

Clue 122: Examine the nuts on the display racks' bolts.
1 point

Clue 123: Then look for classic Mickeys at the ends of the display racks.
1 point

Clue 124: Now check out the bolt ends themselves.
2 points

Clue 125: Observe the gauges on the wall.
1 point

Clue 126: Search for Donald's shadow.
3 points

Clue 127: Spot a set of Hidden Mickey gears.
2 points

Clue 128: Finally, look at the tops of the garment display mannequins.
1 point

★ Walk outside the shop toward *Test Track* and take the first right onto a **walkway leading to World Showcase**.

Clue 129: Stare at the cement as you walk until you discover a Hidden Mickey.
5 points

★ Now cross to the west side of Innoventions Plaza to **Club Cool**.

Clue 130: Study the doors.
4 points

★ Now walk past Fountainview Ice Cream to **Epcot Character Spot** and then walk on through the front entrance.

Clue 131: Look above the entrance doors for a Hidden Mickey.
3 points

Clue 132: Search for Mickey's hat in four different places in and around *Character Spot*.
5 points for spotting all four

Clue 133: Find Goofy and his Hidden Mickey.
3 points

Clue 134: Look around for a yellow classic Mickey made of buttons.
3 points

Clue 135: Spot Mickey's gloves.
2 points

Clue 136: Don't miss Mickey in the stars!
3 points

Clue 137: Find Mickey's ears.
1 point

Clue 138: Search for Mickey in the clouds.
3 points

★ Stroll inside **Innoventions West**.

Clue 139: Search for a classic Mickey in freckles.
3 points

Total Points for Epcot =

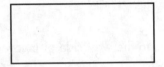

How'd you do?
Up to 188 points - Bronze
189 - 377 points - Silver
378 points and over - Gold
472 points - Perfect Score

(If you earned bonus points in the *Test Track* photo selection area and/or outside the miniature train exhibit in Germany, you may have done even better!)

**Caution:
Don't peek at this
section unless you
really want help!**

The Land Pavilion

- *Soarin'*

Hint 1: Along the right side of the entrance queue, five screens show changing artistic landscapes. In the landscape with the purple mountain ridge in the lower background, a large green tree halfway up the right side of the screen hosts a classic Mickey group of flowers.

Hint 2: In the pre-show video, a man has his Mickey Mouse ears on, then is asked to take them off.

Hint 3: In the pre-show video, a boy sitting in his ride seat is wearing a red shirt with a Grumpy logo and shorts sporting Mickey Mouse.

Hint 4: On the ride, when you soar over the hills and spot a golf course, look immediately to your lower left and find a golf cart. The man standing on the other side of the cart is holding a blue Mickey balloon.

Hint 5: Now look to the right side of the golf course. About halfway along the fairway is a slightly distorted shadow classic Mickey on the green grass formed by a cluster of three trees. The "ears" of the shadow Mickey touch the right side of the white cart path.

Hint 6: Look straight ahead and then down to the golf course. Spot the man who is about to swing a golf club. When he strikes the golf ball, it will head directly toward you. Watch the ball's rotation to see the dark classic Mickey on the surface of the ball.

Hint 7: As you complete your *Soarin'* ride over Disneyland, the second burst of fireworks forms a huge classic Mickey in the sky.

Mission: SPACE

Hint 8: On the far right and left (outer) video monitors in the Mission Control room, classic Mickey circles appear on the lower part of the surface of Mars.

Hint 9: Continue to watch the video loops as three "status lights" form a classic Mickey at the lower right side of the rightmost monitor screen.

Hint 10: During the video loop on either of the middle monitors, three small waveform images merge into a classic Mickey on the lower left of the screen.

Hint 11: You'll see identical faint classic Hidden Mickeys above a horizontal bar on both sides of the launch door before it opens and before you see the sky.

Hint 12: As your spacecraft is landing on Mars, look sharp for a classic Mickey made of satellite dishes on top of the second building from the end, on the right side of the landing strip.

Hint 13: In the Expedition Mars section of the exit exhibit area, you'll find small classic Mickeys in the design of the video-game joystick consoles at the upper left and upper right corners.

Hint 14: In the center of the gift shop near the exit doors, a large side profile of Mick-

ey Mouse is painted on the ceiling in the middle square.

Hint 15: At either side of Mickey's side profile on the ceiling are side profiles of Donald Duck and Pluto (or is it Goofy?).

Hint 16: In the mural behind the gift shop's cash register, look for Minnie Mouse. There's a small classic Mickey in the dirt under her left foot.

Hint 17: On the left side of the mural behind the gift shop's cash register, spot an upside-down classic Mickey on the lower part of the moon.

Hint 18: The bases of the some merchandise stands near the gift shop exit contain "support arches" in the shape of Mickey.

Hint 19: You'll find Hidden Mickeys on both sides of the exit door from the gift shop in the electrical tubing on the wall. You'll find a classic Mickey on one side and both a side-profile Mickey and a classic Mickey on the other.

- in the entrance plaza

Hint 20: Spot three craters that approximate a classic Mickey at the upper left of the Luna 8 landing site on the back side of the moon.

Hint 21: In the middle of a blue tile area, very near and to the left of a gold strip (as you face the attraction), you'll find a tiny tile classic Mickey (black head and blue ears).

Hint 22: A small classic Mickey formed of white tiles is toward the bottom of a blue tile stripe. Look for a black disc in the cement, near the lowest part of the stripe. Mickey is hiding about four feet from the disc as you go toward the Mars planet.

Hint 23: Two more tile or stone classic Mickeys (black head and white ears) lie next to a drain cover, which is in a circle of tiles to the left of the *Mission: SPACE* sign.

Test Track

- in the waiting queue

Hint 24: Across from area 10a, look for a red tool cabinet. A mug on top of it has a Pez dispenser with a Mickey Mouse head. This Mickey can be spotted best from the regular (or "standby," as Disney calls it) and single rider queues.

Hint 25: As the queue lines climb toward the pre-show room (and before you get to it), a white "Crash Test Vehicle" in area 5b sports a small inspection sticker. (It's visible from the single rider and FASTPASS queues.) The sticker, signed by "M. Mouse," is on the front passenger door.

Hint 26: Near knee calibration area 7b, on the left side of the queue, three washers at the edge of a desk (left of center of the desktop) form an upside-down classic Mickey. This image (and the two following images) can best be seen from the FASTPASS and single rider queues.

Hint 27: Above the washer Mickey, there's a photo of three youngsters wearing Santa Mickey hats on the right side of the wall in back of the desk's upper shelf.

Hint 28: A Mickey Mouse doll sits on an upper shelf at the right side of the same desk.

Hint 29: In the first preshow room (the single-riders' room), an orange classic Mickey is on a greaseboard titled "Test Area Notes."

Hint 30: On the lower right side of the bulletin board (next to the greaseboard) in the single-riders' preshow room, the front tire of a diagrammed car has Mickey ears.

Hint 31: On red car S23, a classic Mickey is on the passenger side of the hood. A yellow and black crash-test sticker is the "head," and the "ears" are two black circles.

- during the ride

Hint 32: As you leave the hot room (the first environmental chamber), a classic Mickey is drawn or traced on the back side of the round thermometer hanging above you to the right.

Hint 33: During the "Environmental Test" part of the *Test Track* ride, in the second window of the first office to the right of the ride vehicle, a mug contains a pencil with a classic Mickey outline at the top.

Hint 34: In the first "Environmental Test" office, a classic Mickey drawn with a red Magic Marker appears on the lower part of a greaseboard on the rear wall. From time to time, you may be able to spot more than one classic Mickey on this board.

Hint 35: As you enter the cold room, a white classic Mickey is high up way back on the left side of the rear wall (not the left side wall, the rear wall that you just came through). You must look back to see it.

Hint 36: In the second window of the second "Environmental Test" office to the right of the ride vehicle, a Mickey Mouse plush doll is sitting with its back against the window.

Hints 37 & 38: Just past the office, you have to look quickly to the right, then the left as you enter the "Corrosion Chamber" to spot two classic Mickeys on auto parts that are just inside the room. Look for a hanging car door to the right and a truck fender to the left. Both sport classic Mickey rust spots.

Hint 39: Just past the near crash with the big truck, a white car sitting to your right has a classic Mickey traced in the dirt on its hood.

Hint 40: As you approach the crash barrier wall, a white car (to the left of and facing

91

the ride vehicle) has a classic Mickey on its open gas tank door. It is formed by three crash-test stickers.

Hint 41: Just before the crash barrier wall, look to the floor on your left to try to spot hoses coiled to form a classic Mickey.

This Hidden Mickey is hard to spot because you are moving so fast. But you can see it on the *Test Track* photo monitors (see below) if you miss it during the ride.

- after the ride

Hint 42: At the *Test Track* photo selection area, check the monitors to see the hoses coiled like classic Mickeys. You'll find them in the upper right area of the photos. If the hoses are not visible on the video monitors, check out the framed photo on the wall just before the photo viewing area.

Hint for possible bonus points: Also on the *Test Track* monitors, you can sometimes spot a car tire and two hubcaps forming a classic Mickey on the floor behind the car.

Hint 43: Just past the photo viewing area and across from the Die Press is Mickey's face on a sticker on the second locker from the left.

Hint 44: In the last red locker on the right, a worn name tag for "John" has Mickey's shoes and red shorts still visible. The tag is on the top shelf of the locker, in the lap of a white teddy bear wearing sunglasses.

Odyssey Center

Hint 45: In the Odyssey Center building, classic Mickeys are in the carpet inside the doors that are nearest the bridge to the *Test Track* area. The largest circles are the "heads," and the smaller circles next to them form the "ears" of classic Mickeys.

Norway Pavilion

- *Maelstrom*

Hint 46: On the left side of the large loading-area mural, a Viking in a ship wears Mickey ears. He's sitting below the middle red stripe of the sail.

Hint 47: Toward the right side of the same mural, a woman cruise director holds a clipboard. To the left of the top of her clipboard, the creases in her white shirt form a side profile of Mickey's face. His face is slightly distorted and he's looking to your left.

Hint 48: Inside the stave church, King Olaf II has a dark classic Mickey embroidered on his tunic near his right thigh.

Mexico Pavilion

- *Gran Fiesta Tour Starring the Three Caballeros*

Hint 49: At the loading area and along the boat ride, banners are strung overhead. Some of the banners resemble three-circle classic Mickeys, with a smiling sun figure as Mickey's head.

Hint 50: At the beginning of the boat ride, smoke rises from the volcano. Every half minute or so, holes in the smoke form classic Mickeys that quickly disappear.

Hint 51: About halfway through the ride, in the small blue pond to the left of the boat, classic Mickeys appear in the bubbles after Donald is taken away. Look above and also to the lower left of the octopus.

Hint 52: Toward the end of the ride, as you enter the fireworks room, three drums form a classic Hidden Mickey at the lower right of the "Viva Donald" barge to the left of your boat.

- San Angel Inn Restaurant

Hint 53: Smoke rising from the volcano by the river forms classic Mickeys that quickly disappear.

China Pavilion

Hint 54: Classic Mickey-shaped flowers are sculpted on the bases of several decorative light posts on the outside front of the pavilion.

Hint 55: On the huge white flat sculpted stone near the entrance to the Temple of Heaven, the second group of swirls from the lower right (as you face the temple) resembles an upside down classic Mickey.

Germany Pavilion

Hint 56: On the second floor of the building to your right, to the right of the glockenspiel clock, are three suits of armor. The one closest to the glockenspiel has a classic Mickey on its crown.

Hint 57: In the rear of the courtyard, a three-circle classic Mickey formation is in the ironwork support behind the bell on the front of the clock tower.

- around the miniature train exhibit

Hint 58: A shrub shaped like a classic Mickey is near the small town at the front of the exhibit, close to the center walkway.

Italy Pavilion

Hint 59: In the wine shop, Enoteca Castello, classic Mickey holes are in the woodwork at the left front of the wine counter.

American Adventure Pavilion

Hint 60: A picture on a first-floor wall at the right rear of the rotunda (indoors) shows workers building a skyscraper. The tops of two vertical beams behind the workers sport classic Mickeys.

Hint 61: On the rear wall of the rotunda, first and second floors, large bronze eagle reliefs have classic Mickeys in the corners.

- The American Adventure Show

Hint 62: At the beginning of the film, a classic Mickey appears on the rock behind (and to your right of) a kneeling female pilgrim.

Hint 63: Early in the show, a classic Mickey lock hangs on the right side of a stockade in a scene of the American Revolution time period.

Hint 64: At the end of the show, fireworks light up the sky behind the Statue of Liberty Torch as it rises from the floor. One of the last fireworks at the upper right fizzles into a classic Mickey head (best seen from the right side of the theater).

- Fife and Drums Corps

Hint 65: Four classic Mickeys appear on the Fife and Drums Corps drums. A black one is on the lower front of the big bass drum. Three more decorate the smaller snare drum: two black (one on each side of the lower part of the drum) and a small blue one (traced on a blue banner on the right rear middle).

Japan Pavilion

Hint 66: In the koi fish pond across from the Mitsukoshi store, a drain cover in the water near the bamboo fence sports a classic Mickey.

Hint 67: The trees in the courtyard are encircled by metal grates with classic Mickey designs.

Hint 68: At the rear of the Yakitori House, near the drinking fountain in the outdoor seating area, three short bamboo poles form a classic Mickey when viewed from above.

Hint 69: A classic Mickey formed by three

rocks is deep inside a hole in a large bush. It's on the right side of the pavilion, next to the far right sidewalk to the Mitsukoshi store and near a juniper tree.

Morocco Pavilion

Hint 70: Three brass plates are arranged to form a classic Mickey on the left green door at the entrance to the Souk-Al-Magreb "Gifts of Morocco" shop on the promenade. (Sometimes, the plates are on the nearby red door.)

Hint 71: Across from Restaurant Marrakesh, three small classic Mickeys are on a mural on the rear wall of a small room. One is at the top of a tower on the right side of the mural's street. Another is on the left side of the street, next to a double archway. The third is a tiny black Mickey in an upper doorway on the left middle part of the mural.

France Pavilion

Hint 72: The trees in the courtyard are encircled by metal grates with classic Mickey patterns.

Hint 73: In the patterned hedge (parterre) garden, a bush in the middle right area (on the side nearest the canal) is trimmed to the shape of a classic Mickey.

Hint 74: On the right side of the pavilion, enter a small room from the walkway between shops. Across the room to your right (the Librairie et Galerie room), a book on a top shelf has a classic Mickey worn into the upper spine.

Hint 75: Classic Mickey images are high on the outside molding of Les Vins de France shop, near the entrance to *Impressions de France*.

- *Impressions de France*

Hint 76: In the movie's outdoor wedding scene, you can see a Mickey head and ears in a second floor window, center screen, of the house in the background.

United Kingdom Pavilion

Hint 77: Outside the Sportsman's Shoppe, a sign has a classic Mickey with a tennis racket head, a soccer ball for one ear and a rugby ball for the other.

Canada Pavilion

Hint 78: Past the steps into the pavilion, the left totem pole has black classic Mickeys on both sides near the top by the raven's beak.

Hint 79: A small black classic Mickey is on the side of a fish, which is hanging on the outside of a box at the left rear of the first room as you enter the Northwest Mercantile shop.

Hint 80: Behind the check-in desk at Le Cellier Steakhouse, three horizontal bottles at the center top of a wine display form a classic Mickey.

The Seas with Nemo & Friends Pavilion

Hint 81: Along the inside entrance queue for the ride, a classic Mickey made of moving water circles is hanging from the ceiling in the far right corner as you reach the wooden rails along the walkway.

Hint 82: On the ride, a classic Mickey impression in rock lies below the fifth video screen from the start. It's slightly above and between two pink clusters of standing corals, to the right of center in the rock ledge.

Hint 83: A classic Mickey formed of rocks is at the bottom of the aquarium. It's best seen from the fourth window on the right as you enter the corridor leading to the circular viewing area upstairs. (Warning: this rock Mickey may change locations on the aquarium floor. You may need to look through several windows in the observation area to find it.)

Hint 84: In the manatee viewing room, lower level, bubbles in wall paintings form two classic Mickeys. One is on the left wall (as you exit), in the left middle square that has the words "Manatee Zone … Slow Speed." Another is on the right wall as you exit, in the lower left square with the polar bear.

Hint 85: As you enter Bruce's room on the lower level, an oyster containing three pearls arranged as a classic Mickey is at the lower right of the second window on the right ("Did You Know?"). A similar oyster with classic Mickey pearls is in the second window on the left (labeled "Bruce's Scrapbook").

Hint 86: In the waiting room for "Turtle Talk with Crush," a tiny classic Mickey is in the pink and brown coral in the first window painting to the right as you enter the room. At the lower part of the painting, the Mickey is left of the third tallest (leftmost) blue tube, about one quarter of the distance up the side of the tube.

Hint 87: Bubbles come together and form several classic Mickeys on the garbage cans you see in the pavilion.

The Land Pavilion

- Living with the Land

Hint 88: In the middle section of the giant wall mural at the rear of the queue, bubbles align to form a classic Mickey, ears angled to the left.

Hint 89: A classic Mickey is formed by shrubs (the "head" has yellow dots on it) to the right of the brim of the farmer's hat near the top of the loading dock mural.

Hint 90: In the lower right area of the mural behind the boat loading area, three circles form a small classic Mickey (a purple circle forms the head and blue circles form the ears). The head is tilted slightly to the right.

Hint 91: In the first part of the ride, a female Cast Member on the last video screen on

your left has a Mickey Mouse face on the upper left part of her name tag.

Hint 92: A green garden hose is coiled into a classic Mickey to the right of the boat about halfway through the fish farming section. (Cast Members usually place this Mickey image every morning.)

Hint 93: Plants of different colors are usually arranged to form classic Mickeys in the greenhouses. Often the plants are lettuces.

Hint 94: Toward the end of the ride, a large circular test tube holder on the right side of a laboratory room has a green classic Mickey head in the center.

Hint 95: Near the end of the ride, on the left side of the boat, a small classic Mickey is in the clouds in the middle of planet Earth.

- The Garden Grill restaurant

Hint 96: On the left side of the large wall mural of vegetation is a Mickey hiding behind the most prominent fern that extends all the way to the top. Counting up horizontally from the bottom of the fern, his face is mostly behind the fifth through eighth leaves on the fern's right side. He's looking slightly downward and to the right in a three-quarter profile. Two black circles that form his eyes are visible above the sixth fern leaf on the right, more than halfway to the end of the leaf. Mickey's ears jut above the seventh leaf, and his mouth and nose are below the sixth leaf. His face and ears are green, and his mouth is slightly open. This Hidden Mickey is a real classic!

Hint 97: In the restaurant, Chip and Dale wear red bandannas with small, dark classic Mickeys in the design.

- main entrance to The Land Pavilion

Hint 98: From the upper level railing, just to the left as you walk in the main entrance, a classic Mickey is on the Earth above the lobby. It's in water swirls, to the left of the tip of South America.

Hint 99: A classic Mickey is in the mosaic mural on the right wall outside as you enter the Land Pavilion. Find the word "LAND" on the mural and look slightly above and to the right about six feet or so to a reddish plateau. Just above the left side of the flat upper part of the plateau are three jewels, a green "head" and two reddish "ears."

Hint 100: About halfway along the "Behind the Seeds" tour in the greenhouses, an electrical box on the right side of the tour path sports a photo of a lettuce classic Mickey. You may have spotted one similar to it during the *Living with the Land* ride; see clue and hint 93.

Imagination! Pavilion

- Journey Into Imagination with Figment

Hint 101: In the center of the Sight Room, headphones on the left of two tables have Mickey ears on an ear-piece!

Hint 102: Three bubbles make a classic Mickey near Figment's hand on the edge of his bathtub.

Hint 103: In Figment's Upside-Down House, his toilet forms a classic Mickey with two red circles on the floor.

Hint 104: When you feel a blast of air and the walls open, you'll see a rainbow and balloons. Look down and to the right to see classic Mickey circles appear on a cloud at the bottom right of the stage

Hint 105: On the left wall of the exit hallway, a side-ways classic Mickey is behind and between the "I" and "m" of the "ImageWorks" sign.

- ImageWorks

Hint 106: In *ImageWorks*, an eye chart on the wall in the first scene to your left as you exit the ride has a classic Mickey on line 5.

Hint 107: Behind a pillar in the middle of *Image-Works*, a classic Hidden Mickey is on the floor made of tan colored tile.

Spaceship Earth

Hint 108: The mural to the right of the entrance walkway includes a rocket with an ID number on its side. You'll find Mickey's ears inside the circles of the number "3."

Hint 109: After the fall of Rome, you see three Islamic scholars seated around a table on the floor. They are illuminated by lights that form patterns on the floor. The outer circle of light patterns form classic Mickeys.

Hint 110: After the fall of Rome, a wall with books and scrolls on shelves appears to your left. In one of the last cubbyholes before you leave the scene, about halfway up the wall, there are three horizontal scrolls whose ends form a classic Mickey.

Hint 111: During the ride, in a scene to the left, monks are writing at desks. In front of the sleeping monk is a document with a small ink blot at the upper right corner. The blot is shaped like a classic Mickey and becomes visible as your vehicle passes by.

Hint 112: Just after the Gutenberg printing press scene, in the first part of the Renaissance section, look for the first painter to the left of your ride vehicle. Three white paint circles form a classic Mickey on the top left of the table near the painter. You have to look fast for this one.

Hint 113: On the right side, as you're passing the section showing black and white movies, a chalkboard marquee on the ground lists upcoming features. One is "The Band Concert," a famous Mickey Mouse cartoon.

Hint 114: As soon as you enter the large computer room, look to the right of your vehicle to spot an orange mug on a desk.

101

HINTS HINTS HINTS HINTS HINTS HINTS HINTS HINTS HINTS HINTS HINTS HINTS

You'll see one side of a Mickey Mouse sticker on the mug. As you pass by the desk, look back to your right into the large mirror at the rear of the room. You can see the full Mickey sticker on the mug!

Hint 115: Just past the large computer room, a Mickey Mouse sticker is on the bottom left of the rear window, driver's side, of a red car to the left of the ride vehicle.

Hint 116: Another Mickey Mouse sticker is on the rear wall of the garage, just to the right of the middle of the window.

Hint 117: At the exit of *Spaceship Earth*, several classic Mickeys float along on overhead blue screens in the Project Tomorrow interactive area.

Universe of Energy

Hint 118: After the dinosaur section of the ride, the movie shows a man driving a car out of a barn and towards a church building in the background (the fourth building from the left). A shadow of the Disney's Hollywood Studios's "Earful" Tower appears in the door of the church.

Tip Board in Innoventions Plaza

Hint 119: Australia is shaped like a classic Mickey on the rotating Earth that forms the "O" in Epcot.

Innoventions

- Innoventions East

Hint 120: On the wall maps inside the various entrance doors, a classic Mickey computer mouse is the icon for area number 9.

- Mouse Gear shop

Hint 121: The signs above the shop entrances have classic Mickeys with two round ears above the letter "G" as the head.

Hint 122: The large wing nuts on the bolts of the display racks form Mickey ears.

Hint 123: At the ends of some of the display racks, bolts next to larger holes form classic Mickeys.

Hint 124: The ends of some of the large bolts that jut out from the stippled panels on the merchandise cases are stamped with classic Mickeys.

Hint 125: Some of the gauges on the wall are arranged as classic Mickeys.

Hint 126: The shadows of Donald Duck and his relatives are on the upper part of a wall in the center of the store.

Hint 127: Classic Mickey gears hang above a display on a wall opposite the cash registers.

Hint 128: Some of the garment display mannequins have classic Mickeys at the top.

Hint 129: Outside and behind Mouse Gear is a classic Mickey in the walkway cement. Exit the shop at the rear heading toward *Test Track*, then take the first right onto a walkway (heading toward World Showcase). Just before the path changes to an octagonal shape, look down near the left railing to find a small classic Mickey indented in the concrete.

- Club Cool

Hint 130: In the Innoventions West building, the rear door of Club Cool (facing the Imagination! Pavilion) has a classic Mickey formed of solid circles that come together on the right side (as you face Club Cool) when the door is open.

- Character Spot

Hint 131: In the *Character Spot*, a small white classic Mickey is on the inside wall among the stars above the entrance doors, to the upper right of the exit sign.

Hint 132: A Mickey hat appears in several places: near the right end of the inside wall mural in the waiting queue, outside on window murals near the entrance doors and over the exit doors, and on the outdoor sign, where it is behind and below the "CH" on the side of the sign that faces the Land Pavilion.

Hint 133: Goofy is on an upper inside window, across from the second greeting bay. There's a small, white classic Mickey on his spacesuit.

Hint 134: The yellow buttons on a giant cell phone on the right side of the middle greeting bay form a classic Mickey.

Hint 135: Mickey's gloves are on a robot light switch in the next to last greeting bay.

Hint 136: A constellation classic Mickey is on the right rear wall of the last greeting bay.

Hint 137: In the last bay on the right, a green alien wears Mickey Mouse ears.

Hint 138: A side-profile cloud Mickey floats in the sky mural on an upper inside window across from the last greeting bay.

- Innoventions West

Hint 139: In the postcards area, near the end of the third wall from the right, a boy with a red fez has blue freckles on his face that form a classic Mickey.

CHAPTER 4

Disney's Hollywood Studios Scavenger Hunt

Note: Many of the Hidden Mickeys in this park are in restaurants and shops. Be considerate of fellow guests and Cast Members as you search. Tell them what you are looking for, so they can share in the fun. Avoid searching restaurants at busy meal times unless you are one of the diners.

★ Your scavenger hunt in Disney's Hollywood Studios (aka "the Studios") starts even **before you enter** the park.

Clue 1: Look closely at the brackets on the signs above the ticket windows.
2 points

Clue 2: Examine the fence at the entrance turnstiles.
1 point

★ Walk first to **Toy Story Midway Mania!**

Clue 3: Find a blue classic Mickey along the standby entrance queue.
5 points

Clue 4: On the ride, don't miss classic Mickeys on a Ferris wheel!
5 points

Clue 5: Stay alert for a classic Mickey below an exclamation point on the wall.
5 points

Clue 6: Along the exit walkway, spot a classic Mickey on a wall.
2 points

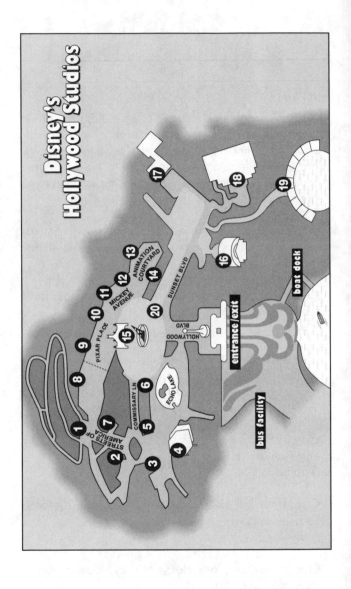

1. Lights, Motors, Action!™ Extreme Stunt Show
2. MuppetVision 3-D
3. Star Tours
4. Indiana Jones™ Epic Stunt Spectacular
5. Sounds Dangerous — Starring Drew Carey
6. The American Idol Experience
7. "Honey, I Shrunk the Kids" Movie Set Adventure
8. Studio Backlot Tour
9. Toy Story Midway Mania!
10. Journey Into Narnia
11. Walt Disney: One Man's Dream
12. Voyage of The Little Mermaid
13. The Magic of Disney Animation
14. Playhouse Disney — Live on Stage!
15. The Great Movie Ride
16. "Beauty and the Beast" — Live on Stage
17. Rock 'n' Roller Coaster® Starring Aerosmith
18. The Twilight Zone Tower of Terror™
19. Fantasmic!
20. Guest Information Board

Clue 7: Study a book along the exit for a tiny classic Mickey.
5 points

★ Now go to **Rock 'n' Roller Coaster Starring Aerosmith**. (You can find the Hidden Mickeys here without riding the coaster, the first nine by exiting before the ride, two in the gift shop by walking in through the exit from outside, and three outside in the courtyard.)

Clue 8: Look down at the carpet along the entrance queue for Hidden Mickeys.
4 points

Clue 9: Don't miss the tiny Mickey on a wall poster just before the pre-show room.
4 points

Clue 10: Search the pre-show room for a classic Mickey.
4 points

Clue 11: After the pre-show, find three Mickeys on a poster.
4 points for spotting all three

Clue 12: Before boarding, spot two Mickeys near the ceiling.
4 points for spotting both

Clue 13: At the loading gate, look at the rear license plates of the limo ride vehicles. (Then exit if you wish.)
4 points

Clue 14: At the exit, find a box with a classic Mickey. (If you haven't taken the ride, walk in through the gift shop to the video monitor area to find this Mickey.)
4 points

Clue 15: In the gift shop, spot a Hidden Mickey on the wall.
3 points

Clue 16: Outside in the courtyard, search for three Hidden Mickeys on the wall.
5 points for spotting all three

★ Walk to the **Twilight Zone Tower of Terror** and explore the entry queue area and pre-show for three Hidden Mickeys.

Clue 17: During the pre-show film in the library, find the plush Mickey Mouse doll held by a little girl.
3 points

Clue 18: Linger in the left library to spot the words "Mickey Mouse" on sheet music on a desktop.
4 points

Clue 19: Notice a classic Mickey stain on the wall in the boiler room.
4 points

Tip: For the best vantage point for the ride Hidden Mickeys, take the right queue when the line for the ride splits. Then tell the Cast Member you're hunting for Hidden Mickeys and ask to be seated in the right-most ride vehicle.

Clue 20: At the first stop on the ride, search for a Hidden Mickey above you.
4 points

Clue 21: Also look for a Mickey Mouse doll here.
4 points

Clue 22: Stare at the star field (the doors to the elevator shaft just before they open!) for a Hidden Mickey in the stars.
5 points

Clue 23: After you leave your elevator, keep alert for a classic Mickey near the photo selection area.
3 points

Clue 24: As you exit, spot Mickey on the floor!
4 points

★ Walk down Sunset Boulevard and turn right to **The Great Movie Ride**. First find two classic Mickeys among the celebrity impressions in the cement in front of the Chinese Theater, and then take the ride.

(If the wait is more than 15 minutes, go on to *Star Tours* and try this later. Best times: during a parade or two hours before park closing.)

Clue 25: Check Harry Anderson's square.
3 points

Clue 26: Now see if you can spot a Mickey in Carol Burnett's square.
3 points

Clue 27: In the middle of the loading dock mural, search for the Hidden Minnie above a tree stump.
Tip: It's visible at loading and unloading.
5 points

Clue 28: On the right side of this mural, squint for a tiny black Hidden Mickey.
5 points

Clue 29: As you start down Gangster Alley, look for Mickey's brown shoes under a James Cagney poster.
4 points

Clue 30: At the end of Gangster Alley, find Mickey's shadow in a window near the top of the "Chemical Company" building.
5 points

Clue 31: In the "Raiders of the Lost Ark" scene, stare to the right of your vehicle for a small white classic Mickey on a tablet below the ark container. It's near a snake.
5 points

Clue 32: Find Mickey and Donald on the left wall, at the end of the "Raiders of the Lost Ark" scene. Psst! Mickey is facing Donald.
5 points

Clue 33: Look up to spot Mickey in the trees in the "Wizard of Oz" set.
5 points

★ Outside the exit, walk past the Sorcerer's Hat and turn right (with Echo Lake on your left) to **Star Tours**. Catch four Hidden Characters along the outside and inside entrance queue and a fifth in the pre-boarding instructional video. You can exit before the ride if you prefer to focus on the scavenger hunt.

(If the line is too long, use the FASTPASS option if it's available to you.)

Clue 34: Don't miss a classic Mickey on a tree along the outside queue.
5 points

Clue 35: Wave at Mickey on the right as you enter the building.
2 points

Clue 36: Look for another Hidden Mickey near the building entrance.
3 points

Clue 37: Marvel at a Hidden Kermit the Frog on the right side of the entrance queue.
4 points

Clue 38: Keep an eye out for an Ewok taking his seat in the *Star Tours* instructional video.
2 points

Clue 39: Find a classic Mickey in the gift shop at the exit.
3 points

★ Catch the next **Lights, Motors, Action! Extreme Stunt Show**.

Clue 40: Don't miss classic Mickeys along the entrance walkway.
4 points for two

Clue 41: Search for a small full body Mickey Mouse at the rear of the set.
5 points

Clue 42: Find a classic Mickey in a set window.
5 points

★ Take a lunch break. Keep your priority seating reservations if you have them. If not, try the Backlot Express for burgers and sandwiches, the Toy Story Pizza Planet for pizza, or the ABC Commissary for salads and stir-fry.

★ Check your Times Guide for convenient shows of *The American Idol Experience* and *Beauty and the Beast*. While you're seated, **check your Studios park map** for a Hidden Mickey.

Clue 43: Turn the Disney's Hollywood Studios park map upside down and search for Mickey.
4 points

★ After lunch, go to **MuppetVision 3-D** and find five Hidden Mickeys.

Clue 44: Look for a Mickey Mouse in the fountain outside *MuppetVision*.
2 points

Clue 45: On the wall near the far turn of the long outside waiting queue, check out the poster about 3-D glasses to find a classic Mickey.
3 points

Clue 46: Observe the test pattern during the first part of the pre-show on the video monitors.
4 points

Clue 47: Near the end of the main show, find the classic Mickey on band members' Colonial-style hats.
4 points

Clue 48: Try to spot the Mickey balloons after Kermit rides in on a fire truck.
3 points

★ Walk up the Streets of America. Turn right and pass by the *"Honey I Shrunk the Kids" Movie Set Adventure* to the **Studio Backlot Tour**. Find three classic Mickeys as you tour the backlot.

Clue 49: Don't miss a drawing of Walt Dis-

ney and two images of Mickey Mouse on the wall.
3 points for spotting all three images

Clue 50: Search for Mickey's gloves and shoes in the prop storage area.
3 points for spotting both

Clue 51: Look closely at the refrigerator on the right side of the first aisle in the prop storage area.
3 points

Caution: If the waiting queue is short, you may bypass the winding aisles. If you do, look down the first aisle to spot the fridge, or step past the ropes to explore the first aisle away from the crowds.

Clue 52: While on the tram, stay alert for a classic Mickey on a shelf inside a window.
4 points

Clue 53: While on the tram, spot a classic Mickey on an airplane.
3 points

Clue 54: Study a mural in the exit displays (after the tram ride) for three Mickey images.
5 points for spotting all three

★ Walk to *Studio Catering Co.*

Clue 55: Search for a Hidden Mickey on a wall.
3 points

Clue 56: Find three classic Mickeys on the trailer.
4 points for spotting all three

★ Walk down Mickey Avenue to *Walt Disney: One Man's Dream*.

Clue 57: During your walk through the attraction, look around for a Hidden Donald near Walt, who is holding a pointer.
3 points

Clue 58: Now find a Hidden Mickey on the wall near Walt.
3 points

113

Clue 59: Search for Donald and three Mickey images near the Animatronics robot.
5 points for finding all four images

★ Continue down Mickey Avenue, then up the steps or through the arch, and veer left to **The Hollywood Brown Derby** restaurant. Admire the mural on the wall outside, above the restaurant.

Clue 60: Look for two classic Mickeys in the mural.
4 points for spotting both

★ Now look at the pictures in the waiting area inside the restaurant.

Clue 61: Spot the man with Mickey Mouse ears.
3 points

★ Catch a performance of **The American Idol Experience**.

Clue 62: Find Mickey on the stage background.
5 points

★ Turn left as you leave and **head down Sunset Boulevard**.

Clue 63: Search for a classic Mickey in scrollwork on a blue building.
4 points

Clue 64: Look around for Mickey in a café behind the service counter.
3 points

★ Plan to catch a performance of **Beauty and the Beast**. Sit to the right of center in the theater.

Clue 65: Stay alert for a Mickey on a cake.
5 points

Clue 66: Watch for Mickey on the back of one of the characters.
3 points

114

★ Turn left onto Hollywood Boulevard, then right to **Hollywood & Vine restaurant**.

Clue 67: Seek a Hidden Character above the entrance.
3 points

★ Enter the restaurant and examine the left wall.

Clue 68: Find a stick figure Mickey.
2 points

Clue 69: Search the wall for some classic Mickeys.
3 points

★ Step inside the waiting area for the **50's Prime Time Café** and look closely at the tables.

Clue 70: Check out what's holding them together.
1 point

★ Walk to a faux security booth near **Indiana Jones™ Epic Stunt Spectacular!**

Clue 71: Find two Mickeys!
4 points for spotting both

★ Enter the **Backlot Express restaurant**.

Clue 72: Look for standing Mickeys.
4 points for finding four or more

★ Stroll to the **Radio Disney sign** to the left of *Sounds Dangerous*.

Clue 73: Take a good look at the "O."
1 point

★ Ask a restaurant Cast Member to let you check out the **Sci-Fi Dine-In Theater Restaurant** inside.

Clue 74: Find Mickey in the waiting area.
3 points

Clue 75: Study the right rear mural. Look for

Mickey's ears along the treetops. Psst! They're near a tall palm tree.
5 points

Clue 76: Now search for a waving Mickey.
5 points

Clue 77: Stare at a small mosaic mural at the rear of the restaurant for a side profile of Mickey Mouse.
5 points

Clue 78: Watch the movie reel for three Hidden Characters.
8 points for spotting all three

Clue 79: Stay alert for a classic Mickey on a spacesuit.
4 points

Clue 80: Find a Hidden Mickey on a dining car.
3 points

★ Get yourself some coffee or other refreshment at **The Writer's Stop**. Look up while you enjoy it.

Clue 81: See anything on the overhead theater lights?
2 points

Clue 82: Look around for Mickey on the wall.
2 points

★ Mosey over to the **Toy Story Pizza Planet** and find three Hidden Mickeys.

Clue 83: Search for a small classic Mickey in the stars above the counter registers. Focus on the left side of the pizzeria's rear wall.
4 points

Clue 84: Swing your eyes over to the right side of the rear wall to find a bright classic-Mickey star cluster.
3 points

Clue 85: Now find a three-quarter Mickey profile above the arcade games on the wall mural. Psst! He's looking left.
5 points

116

★ Wander into the **Stage 1 Company Store** and find two Hidden Mickeys.

Clue 86: Take a good look at the old bureau that's loaded with hats and paint cans.
3 points

Clue 87: Spot a classic Mickey on the wall.
3 points

Clue 88: Search for some famous shorts.
3 points

Clue 89: Outside the store, look for a purple Mickey.
3 points

★ In the waiting area for **Mama Melrose's Ristorante Italiano**, search for four classic Mickeys.

Clue 90: Check out the Dalmatian.
3 points

Clue 91: Examine the plaster on the right wall.
3 points

Clue 92: Find a classic Mickey leaf near the check-in podium.
4 points

Clue 93: Now look at the plaster on the wall to the left of the check-in podium.
3 points

★ Stroll to **Radiator Springs**, where the Cars characters sign autographs.

Clue 94: Spot a side-profile Mickey.
4 points

★ Walk down the **Streets of America**.

Clue 95: Search for a San Francisco newspaper with a Hidden Mickey.
4 points

Clue 96: Keep looking around for the Incredibles.
3 points

Clue 97: Find a Mickey Mouse watch in a window.
4 points

Clue 98: Don't miss the photo of Walt with Mickey!
4 points

Clue 99: Search for three classic characters in a window near a cruise ship.
4 points for spotting all three

Clue 100: Spot Mickey in the sand in a New York window.
3 points

★ Walk left to the **end of Commissary Lane**, then stop at a faux security booth labeled "Gate 1."

Clue 101: Find Mickey inside the booth.
2 points

★ Walk past *The Great Movie Ride* to the entrance arch to **Animation Courtyard**.

Clue 102: Search the show's entrance area for Hidden Characters.
4 points for finding two characters

★ Enjoy *"The Magic of Disney Animation."*

Clue 103: Watch for Hidden Mickeys on a mug.
4 points

★ Stroll over to Hollywood Boulevard. At the **intersection of Hollywood and Sunset Boulevards**, discover Mickey Mouse's previous moniker.

Clue 104: Read the impressions in the sidewalks, near the curb.
5 points

★ Look at a billboard above the **Keystone Clothiers** shop.

Clue 105: See any handprints in cement?
3 points

Clue 106: Walk behind *Keystone Clothiers* and search for a classic Mickey.
2 points

★ Enter **Mickey's of Hollywood** store to look for four Hidden Mickeys.

Clue 107: Check the posts holding up merchandise racks.
2 points

Clue 108: Now examine the racks themselves.
2 points

Clue 109: Study the cabinets in the Sorcerer section of the store. Tip: They are near a door to the street.
2 points

Clue 110: Next find "MICKEYS" spelled out on vertical dividers.
1 point

★ Go to the **Cover Story store** and take a good look at the outside.

Clue 111: Can you spot the classic Mickeys hiding in the design?
2 points

★ Walk outside the park to the **charter bus area**.

Clue 112: Search for Mickey in the cement next to a bench.
5 points

★ In the evening during the **Fantasmic!** show:

Clue 113: Look for large bubbles floating up the water screen that form a classic Hidden Mickey.
5 points

Total Points
for Disney's Hollywood Studios =

How'd you do?
Up to 162 points - Bronze
163 - 325 points - Silver
326 points and over - Gold
408 points - Perfect Score

**Caution:
Don't peek at this
section unless you
really want help!**

- Park entrance area

Hint 1: Metal brackets at the bottoms of signs above the ticket purchase windows are shaped like classic Mickeys.

Hint 2: You'll see classic Mickeys on top of the fence at the turnstiles.

- Toy Story Midway Mania!

Hint 3: An upside-down blue paint classic Mickey is on the wall past the large map of the U.S.A., below a green dinosaur and an orange fish (Nemo), near the floor and behind the handrails on the left side of the queue.

Hint 4: About halfway along the ride, a carnival mural against the wall has a Ferris wheel with seats that have Mickey ears.

Hint 5: Look for the words "Circus Fun!" on the wall to your right as you rotate into position for the last screen stop. The dot below the exclamation point is a classic Mickey.

Hint 6: On the wall to the left of the ride vehicles, a classic Mickey is formed by three ovals that outline Mr. Potato Head, Slinky Dog, and Bullseye the horse. You can see this image at loading and unloading, and you can study it as you take the exit walkway.

Hint 7: On the upper spine of the large Tin Toy book along the exit, a tiny white classic Mickey is in a chicken's eye. It's the fourth image from the top of the spine.

- Rock 'n' Roller Coaster Starring Aerosmith

Hint 8: Along the entrance queue, when you reach the inner room past the tile floor, distorted classic Mickeys are in the carpet.

Hint 9: On the last wall before you enter the pre-show room, a poster labeled "Cosmic Car Show" has a tiny classic Mickey on the bottom right under the front tire of the car.

Hint 10: Cables coiled into a classic Mickey are on the rear center of the floor in the pre-show room where Aerosmith appears.

Hint 11: You'll find three full-body Mickey Mouse stickers at the upper right and middle right side of a collage poster. The poster is on the wall to your left at the first right turn in the inside queue near the boarding area.

Hint 12: After the right turn in the inside queue near the boarding area, about halfway to the end and above the "Compact Vehicles Only" notation on the wall, the first and third light fixtures near the ceiling sport Mickey stickers.

Hint 13: On the rear license plate of each limo ride vehicle, the year sticker at the upper right is a classic Mickey.

Hint 14: Just as people exit the ride vehicle, look for "Box #15" on the side. The "o" in "Box" is a classic Mickey.

Hint 15: In the gift shop, a "shadow box" display on the wall near the exit walkway holds a classic Mickey formed by black disks.

Hint 16: As you exit into the front courtyard, check the outside wall mural to your left for: a boy wearing Mickey ears, black classic Mickeys on a singer's shirt, and a gold "bling" Mickey on the necklace of the man in the black suit.

- The Twilight Zone Tower of Terror

Hint 17: During the pre-show film in the library, the little girl on the elevator holds a plush Mickey Mouse doll.

Hint 18: Look for sheet music on a desktop and under a trumpet in the left library. The words "Mickey Mouse" are included in a song title.

Hint 19: A black, slightly distorted classic Mickey stains the wall of the boiler room at the spot where the queue branches, about eight feet up from the walkway, between an "Exit" sign and a red electrical box.

Hint 20: At the first stop on the ride, a small, dark classic Mickey can be seen above the ghostly images in the lower center of the ornate design on the closest archway.

Hint 21: Also at this first stop, the little girl in the ghostly images is still holding her Mickey doll.

Hint 22: On the ride itself, you'll see a bright star field just before the doors open into the elevator shaft. Look closely as the stars you're watching converge in the middle into a small classic Mickey shape for a split second. (Tip: You see it best from the rightmost ride vehicle.)

Hint 23: In the room below and behind the screens that show the photo ride images, look to the left to an open drawer for gauges in a drawer that form a classic Mickey.

Hint 24: On the left side of the last room as you exit the ride (and before the gift shop), three distinct floor tiles form a classic Mickey. (It's not proportioned correctly but it is clearly purposeful).

- The Great Movie Ride

Hint 25: Harry Anderson's celebrity impression is at the front left of the Chinese Theater (as you face the entrance). Look for a classic Mickey on Harry's tie.

Hint 26: Four squares to the right of Harry Anderson's impression, Carol Burnett's square has classic Mickey ears in the upper right side.

Hint 27: In the loading dock area, a shadow of Minnie Mouse's head in side profile is visible on the wall mural during loading and unloading. To find it, first spot the house in the middle of the mural. Then look above and to the right of the house to spot Minnie's shadow. She's looking to your left. Having trouble? Look at the ride vehicles. The shadow is to the left of the front section of the second of the two vehicles.

Hint 28: On the right side of the loading dock mural, a tiny black classic Mickey is in the bottom center of a top-floor window on the side of the house nearest the corner. It's the second to last house on the right.

Hint 29: In the first part of Gangster Alley, Mickey Mouse's brown shoes and tail poke out from under a James Cagney poster, "The Public Enemy," on the left side of the ride vehicle.

Hint 30: At the end of Gangster Alley, a silhouette of Mickey in side profile appears in the rightmost window, near the top of the "Chemical Company" building. It's to the rear left of your ride vehicle.

Hint 31: In the "Raiders of the Lost Ark" scene, a small white classic Mickey is on a broken tablet or flat rock which leans against the foundation that the Ark container sits on. Two white men are painted on the side of the container, and the Mickey image is below and between them. It's just to the left of the head of an orange-brown snake.

124

Hint 32: On the left wall, at the end of

the "Raiders of the Lost Ark" scene, Mickey and Donald can be found in the far left corner of the scene. They're facing one another and Mickey is to the right of Donald, on the third row of panes up from the floor.

Hint 33: A classic Mickey is nestled in the top of the trees, midway along the mural above the exit from the "Wizard of Oz" room. The classic Mickey is tilted slightly to the right.

- Star Tours

Hint 34: About halfway along the outside winding queue for *Star Tours*, a white classic Mickey is high on a tree trunk, just below the walkway platform for the Ewok village above. It's on the huge central tree, directly across from the Imperial Walker.

Hint 35: Just inside the building entrance, a Phone Directory on the wall to the right has a full-body Mickey Mouse at the upper left corner.

Hint 36: Just inside the building as you enter, check the left wall for classic Mickey imprints on an "Employment Opportunities" notice at the lower right of a bulletin board.

Hint 37: Along the entrance queue in the room with the moving baskets, wave at Kermit the Frog, who is made from tubes and extra robot parts. He is sitting on the right side of the lower ascending walkway, before it makes a sharp turn to the right.

Hint 38: During the first part of the pre-boarding instructional video, an Ewok carries a plush Mickey Mouse as he moves across the row to his seat on the StarSpeeder. He places the doll under his seat.

Hint 39: At the "Build Your Own Lightsaber" station in the shop at the exit, a classic Mickey is on the front lower right panel. It's formed by bullet holes with surrounding black burn marks as the "ears" and a center raised circle as the "head."

- Lights, Motors, Action! Extreme Stunt Show

Hint 40: Walk through the entrance turnstile and look through the windows of the building on your right. Classic Mickey magnets are stuck on red tool chests behind the first set of windows you encounter and behind the middle set of windows as you turn right at the first corner. These magnet Mickeys change positions on the tool chests at times.

Hint 41: In the right section of the set background, look for a window under an "Antiquities" sign and near a large "Café" sign. A full-body drawing of Mickey Mouse is near a chair in the window's lower right side.

Hint 42: A classic Mickey is behind the upper right windowpane at the rear of the set, under the sign "Motomania."

- Disney's Hollywood Studios park map

Hint 43: The face of Mickey Mouse on the upside-down park map has been distorted over time. The corners of his smile are still visible on both sides of the big Sorcerer's Hat, and his forehead "widow's peak" shows up just below where Hollywood Boulevard ends. (Look closely and you'll see that his smile and widow's peak are darker areas in the cement.) To the right, Echo Lake forms a distorted ear.

- MuppetVision 3-D

Hint 44: In a fountain outside *Muppet-Vision 3-D*, Gonzo is balancing on a character with bulging eyes and face who resembles Mickey Mouse.

Hint 45: On the wall near the far turn of the long outside waiting queue, you'll find a classic Mickey in the center left of a blue poster that says, "5 reasons to return . . . 3-D glasses."

Hint 46: During the first part of the pre-show on the video monitors, a test pattern appears after you see the words "Video Display Test." The black lines on a white background form a classic Hidden Mickey.

126

Hint 47: Near the end of the main show, during the Muppets' celebration with marching bands and fireworks, some of the band members wear blue Colonial-style hats with red tabs on the side. The tabs have classic Mickeys in the center.

Hint 48: After the cannon shoots holes in the theater and Kermit rides in on a firetruck, some of the observers outside are holding Mickey Mouse balloons.

- Studio Backlot Tour

Hint 49: An advertisement with Walt Disney and Mickey Mouse is on a bulletin board behind glass, on the right side of the entrance walkway into the props area. It's in the third display board from the entrance doors. A drawing of Mickey is in the same display, to the left of the purple image of Walt and Mickey.

Hint 50: Along the first aisle, straight ahead in the prop storage building, Mickey's gloves and then his shoes are in the left display area.

Hint 51: On the right side of the first aisle in the movie and TV prop-storage area, the front of a yellow refrigerator sports a silver classic Mickey.

Hint 52: During the initial part of the tram ride, a small wooden partial classic Mickey is on a low shelf just inside a window to the left of your vehicle, near the end of the building that houses the wardrobe and carpentry areas.

Hint 53: Later on the ride, you can see a small classic Mickey image inside the "D" of Disney World on the side of Walt Disney's airplane. The Mickey image on the tail of the plane is decorative, not hidden.

Hint 54: After the tram ride, look for a mural on the right wall just inside the entrance to the AFI display rooms. Just to the left of the tallest building in the mural, in the right center, is a Mickey Mouse statue on a tombstone. Atop the fourth building from the left side of the mural is Mickey's side-profile silhouette. On the right side of the fifth building from the left is a white side profile of his face.

- Studio Catering Co.

Hint 55: At the side of the restaurant, a red classic Mickey lies on a black tile under a fire alarm on the right wall of the High Octane Refreshments Bar.

Hint 56: A large black classic Mickey decorates the hubcap of the "Disney Stars" trailer, and tiny classic and side-profile Mickeys are scattered in the blue background on its side.

- Walt Disney: One Man's Dream

Hint 57: On the left side of the display aisle (and before you are ushered into the theater), you see Walt Disney standing with a pointer in front of a wall map. On a desk to Walt's left, a coffee mug near a telephone has Donald Duck on it.

Hint 58: You can spot a green classic Mickey in the same scene. He's on the wall to the left of Walt.

Hint 59: In one of the last scenes before you reach the theater, four Hidden images are to the left of the Animatronics robot. Donald Duck is on a coffee mug on a desk to the far left; Mickey Mouse is near Donald on a glass with pencils. He's also on the top of a Pez dispenser and on another coffee mug.

- The Hollywood Brown Derby restaurant

Hint 60: Classic Mickeys are in the clouds on the mural on the outside wall above the restaurant. One is at the far upper right of the mural, and another is at the far mid-left of the mural, above the "Stage 5" sign.

Hint 61: On a wall to the left in the waiting area, in the second row of pictures, you'll find a caricature of Jimmy Dodd (with his Mouse ears) from the 1950s' "Mickey Mouse Club" TV show.

- The American Idol Experience

Hint 62: A classic Mickey image is on the light brown arch in the stage backdrop, between the second and third round archway lights (counting from the lower right of the arch).

- Sunset Boulevard

Hint 63: Midway down Sunset Boulevard toward the *Tower of Terror*, the outside scrollwork about halfway to the top of a blue building on the right side of the street has an upside-down classic Mickey in its design.

Hint 64: On the rear wall of Rosie's All-American Café, two regulators form classic Mickeys above the coffee and hot cocoa machines.

- Beauty and the Beast

Hint 65: During the "Be Our Guest" segment, a cart with a large, four-layer cake is wheeled to the right side of the stage (the audience's right). On the front of the cake, a tiny, white classic Mickey is stuck on the second horizontal line of icing from the top. This image is best seen from a seat on the right side of the theater.

Hint 66: A classic Mickey is on the back of Cogsworth. A wind-up device on his back has two holes for the "ears" and a larger circle for the "head." Sometimes this image is upside down.

- Hollywood & Vine restaurant

Hint 67: Outside the restaurant, a silhouette of Roger Rabbit is in a window above and to the left of the entrance.

Hint 68: On the left wall inside, the "San Fernando Valley" wall mural has a stick figure Mickey on the far right, behind a pole.

Hint 69: Bushes form several classic Mickeys to the immediate left and also above the stick figure Mickey.

- 50's Prime Time Café

Hint 70: In the waiting area, washers shaped like classic Mickeys secure the white tabletops.

- near Indiana Jones™ Epic Stunt Spectacular!

Hint 71: There is a security booth (not an actual one) labeled "Gate 2." A full-body Mickey Mouse, along with other characters, is on a coffee mug inside the booth, and Mickey is also drawn at the upper left of a mail tracking sheet. (Note: these images change from time to time.)

Hint 72: Several full-body two-dimensional Mickeys are on the bulletin boards inside the Backlot Express restaurant. One bulletin board is near the exit door facing *Star Tours*. A second is close by at the side of the seating area across from the mural of the city park.

- Radio Disney sign

Hint 73: The "O" in the Radio Disney sign has a classic Mickey in the center.

- Sci-Fi Dine-In Theater Restaurant

Hint 74: Mickey Mouse in a graduation outfit is on an "Educational Reimbursement Program" notice on a bulletin board on a wall in the waiting area.

Hint 75: Face the kitchen, then look to the right of it at the tall fence in the right rear mural. You'll find Mickey's ears in the part of the mural that's above the right section of the fence. Look at the treetops. The Hidden Mickey is part of the outline of the center-right top of a tree that is located to the right of a tall palm tree.

Hint 76: Above the tallest fence to the right of the kitchen, a bush Mickey along the top of the trees is waving with his left hand.

Hint 77: In the multicolored tiles above the kitchen door entrance (on the right as you face the kitchen) is a side profile of Mickey. He is outlined in yellow tiles and appears to

be looking to his left (our right). Look first for his jaw, a curving line of yellow tiles in the middle of the mosaic square.

Hint 78: Watch the movie reel for Donald Duck, Mickey Mouse, and Tinker Bell. Donald is in a cartoon segment about a secretary who is kidnapped to another planet; Donald is one of the characters who chases her. The segment follows a clip of Walt Disney. Mickey appears later in the reel, in a "News of the Future" segment; he wears a spacesuit and waves to the crowd. Tinker Bell flies around above the word "Tomorrowland."

Hint 79: Stay alert for a youngster in a spacesuit during the movie reel, when the words "Calling All Boys! All Girls!" appear on the screen. A classic Mickey formed by a circle and two knobs is on the upper chest of the spacesuit, just below the helmet.

Hint 80: Silver classic Mickeys are at the sides of the car seats, on the running boards.

- The Writer's Stop

Hint 81: Some of the theater lights hanging from the ceiling sport yellow classic Mickeys.

Hint 82: Silver classic Mickeys are in the corners of a wall display on the left rear wall of the store.

- Toy Story Pizza Planet

Hint 83: A classic Mickey is one of the constellations of stars above the counter registers. Focus on the left side of the rear wall, between Woody and the "Disney's Toy Story" sign.

Hint 84: A small, bright classic-Mickey star cluster appears above the counter registers on the right side of the rear wall. Look near the pizza-slice constellation.

Hint 85: Above the arcade games, in the moon near the top of the wall mural, you can spot a three-quarter Mickey profile facing left.

- Stage 1 Company Store

Hint 86: Look for an old bureau that's loaded with hats for sale and has paint cans at the very top. You'll find a green, painted classic Mickey near the center of the desktop.

Hint 87: In the middle of the store, across from the green-paint Hidden Mickey on the bureau, circles in the middle of a cloud at the upper left of a mural with a rainbow form an approximate classic Mickey.

Hint 88: Mickey Mouse's shorts (red with white buttons) are hanging on a line near one of the exit doors.

Hint 89: Outside the store, spilled purple paint forms a classic Mickey on the cement below a lion's head that's on a wall near the exit of the *MuppetVision 3-D* show.

- Mama Melrose's Ristorante Italiano

Hint 90: Just inside the entrance to the right, the Dalmatian has a black classic Mickey spot on its right shoulder (your left).

Hint 91: The right wall between the waiting room and the dining area bears a slightly distorted classic Mickey in the plaster. It's in the upper right corner, near the entrance door.

Hint 92: To the right of the check-in podium (as you face it), a green classic Mickey leaf is about one and a half feet above the bottom of the window, along the left edge.

Hint 93: The left wall between the waiting room and the dining area has a smaller classic Mickey plastered on the brick. You'll find it in the middle left part of the wall, just above the counter.

- The Cars Meet and Greet area

Hint 94: A side profile of Mickey Mouse is etched in the lower part of a side wall to the left of the large brick wall mural that says "Radiator Springs, A Happy Place."

- Streets of America

Hint 95: Some of the newspapers in a newsstand at the left lower area of a mural at the end of San Francisco Street feature articles about Steamboat Willie.

Hint 96: In the lower right and left sides of the same mural, some papers in a small newspaper dispenser feature articles about the Incredibles.

Hint 97: A watch with Mickey on its face is in the window of Sal's Pawn Shop, near the passage to *"Honey I Shrunk the Kids" Movie Set Adventure*.

Hint 98: On the upper left wall of the second window (on the left as you face the Venture Travel Service) is a picture of Walt Disney holding a Mickey Mouse doll in his right hand.

Hint 99: The same window holds three other Hidden Characters: classic Mickey holes decorate the lower edge of a lampshade and in a photo propped on the desk below the shade, Mickey and Minnie are sitting on a bench looking out to a cruise ship at sea. We see just the backs of their heads.

Hint 100: A classic Mickey sand trap is in the leftmost window as you face the New York backdrop at the end of the Streets of America.

- end of Commissary Lane

Hint 101: Mickey Mouse, along with other characters, is on a coffee mug inside the faux security booth. (Note: this mug changes from time to time.)

- Animation Courtyard

Hint 102: Donald Duck and Goofy are etched on the ornamental arches that are adjacent to the main entrance arch to Animation Courtyard.

Hint 103: In the movie during the first part of *The Magic of Disney Animation* tour, a man holds a coffee mug covered with classic Mickeys.

- Intersection of Hollywood & Sunset Blvds.

Hint 104: On both sides of Sunset Boulevard near its intersection with Hollywood Boulevard, you'll find small impressions in the cement sidewalks, near the curb. They read, "Mortimer & Co, 1928 Contractors." Mortimer Mouse was Mickey Mouse's first (and soon discarded) name; 1928 was the year he was "born."

- Keystone Clothiers

Hint 105: Outside and above the shop, a Kodak billboard shows a girl bending forward, partially covering Mickey Mouse's handprints impressed in cement.

Hint 106: Behind the *Keystone Clothiers* shop, at *Peevy's Polar Pipeline* drink service, gauges or regulators form a classic Mickey, especially when viewed from behind.

- Mickey's of Hollywood

Hint 107: Classic Mickey holes are drilled in some of the metal support poles.

Hint 108: The caps on the ends of some merchandise racks are shaped like classic Mickeys.

Hint 109: In the Sorcerer section of the store, near a door to the street, you'll find cabinets with classic Mickey shapes on them.

Hint 110: "MICKEYS" is spelled out on four vertical dividers (two on each side of the store) that separate the sections of the store.

- Cover Story store

Hint 111: You'll find a design containing classic Mickeys on the outside of the store, next to The Darkroom. Look below the second-floor windows.

- near the charter bus area

Hint 112: Outside the park, near the charter bus area, a classic Mickey is stamped in cement. It's about nine or so benches (and three light poles) from the main entrance promenade as you head toward the walkway to the BoardWalk Resort. It's across from the "CG" marker on the cement.

- Fantasmic!

Hint 113: When animated characters float up in large bubbles on the water screen, watch for Pinocchio. His bubble forms the head of a classic Hidden Mickey. Two bubbles beside it form the ears.

Notes

CHAPTER 5

Disney's Animal Kingdom Scavenger Hunt

●●●●●●●●●●●●●●●●●●●●●●●●●

★ Your first stop is **Expedition Everest** in Asia. Walk through the Oasis, turn right in Discovery Island, and follow the path to Asia. Two of the queue Hidden Mickeys are in the FASTPASS line. the rest are in the regular queue, which Disney calls the Standby line because you just walk into it and stand by for the attraction. So get a FASTPASS to use later and then join the Standby queue to search for the Mickeys in Clues 1 through 10.

Clue 1: In the Standby line, search for a classic Mickey in the first sunken courtyard.
3 points

Clue 2: Look around for cloud Hidden Mickeys in a mural.
4 points for spotting both

Clue 3: Keep alert for pipes on a shelf that form a classic Mickey.
3 points

Clue 4: Find a Yeti with Mickey ears.
4 points

Clue 5: Look for a Hidden Mickey made of light-switch devices in a display.
3 points

Clue 6: Stay alert for Mickey on a book.
4 points

Clue 7: Search for Mickey on a handrail.
5 points

Clue 8: Spot a Hidden Mickey in a kettle.
4 points

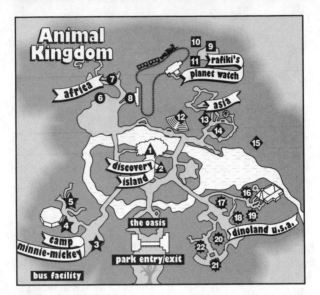

discovery island
1 The Tree of Life
2 It's Tough to be a Bug!

camp minnie-mickey
3 Outdoor Theater
4 Festival of the Lion King
5 Character Greeting Trails

africa
6 Kilimanjaro Safaris
7 Pangani Forest Exploration Trail
8 Train to Rafiki's Planet Watch

rafiki's planet watch
9 Conservation Station
10 Affection Section
11 Habitat Habit!

asia
12 Flights of Wonder
13 Maharajah Jungle Trek
14 Kali River Rapids
15 Expedition Everest

dinoland u.s.a.
16 Finding Nemo – The Musical
17 The Boneyard
18 TriceraTop Spin
19 Primeval Whirl
20 Cretaceous Trail
21 DINOSAUR
22 Dino-Sue T Rex

Clue 9: Squint for a Hidden Mickey paw print.
5 points

Clue 10: Look for an animal with Mickey's ears!
3 points

Clue 11: In the last room before boarding for the Standby and FASTPASS lines, glance around for Sorcerer Mickey.
5 points

Clue 12: In either the FASTPASS or the Single Rider queue, find a Hidden Mickey on a lantern.
4 points

Clue 13: In the loading area outside the FASTPASS line, look for a classic Mickey.
3 points

Clue 14: After the ride starts, stay alert for a classic Mickey melted spot in the snow.
5 points

Clue 15: Find a small classic Mickey in the gift shop at the exit.
3 points

Clue 16: Search outside, near the Serka Zong Bazaar shop, for a classic Mickey.
3 points

Clue 17: Walk around outside the attraction and spot a classic Mickey near a post.
3 points

★ Stroll over to Africa to the **Kilimanjaro Safaris**. Take the ride and look for a classic Mickey in the flamingo pond.

Clue 18: Observe the island in the pond.
4 points

Clue 19: Near the lions, watch for Donald in the rocks.
4 points

★ Visit **DINOSAUR** next. Go back through Discovery Island and follow the walkway into DinoLand. Find a Hidden Mickey on a painting just inside the *DINOSAUR* building.

Clue 20: Can you spot the Mickey on a tree trunk?
4 points

Clue 21: After the ride begins, be alert for a Hidden Mickey on a greaseboard.
4 points

Clue 22: Find a classic Mickey on the red dinosaur in the mural behind the counter in the ride's photo-purchase area.
4 points

★ Walk into the queue for **It's Tough to be a Bug!** on Discovery Island.

Clue 23: When you get inside *The Tree of Life*, look for a Hidden Mickey above the handicapped entrance doors.
4 points

★ Go to **Kali River Rapids** in Asia and find a classic Mickey formed by plates on the wall of one of the rooms you pass through on your way to the ride.

Clue 24: You're getting close when you see stone statues in the grass.
2 points

★ Stroll to the **Maharajah Jungle Trek**. At the tiger exhibit area, find seven classic Hidden Mickeys in the building with arches.

Clue 25: Check in the water in the painting to the right of the first arch.
2 points

Clue 26: Look for the earring Mickey on the left mural inside the first arch.
2 points

Clue 27: Find a leaf Mickey on the left mural inside the first arch.
2 points

Clue 28: Search the right mural inside the first arch for a Hidden Mickey on a man.
2 points

Clue 29: Inside the building with arches, on the right wall, check the flowers on two square panels to find classic Mickeys.
2 points for one or more

Clue 30: Look for a classic Mickey in the mountains inside the second arch.
2 points

Clue 31: Now find a classic Mickey in the cloud formation inside the same arch.
2 points

Clue 32: After you exit the temple ruins, search for a Hidden Mickey in the leaves to your left.
5 points

Clue 33: Walk left toward the nearby animal viewing area and look around for a Mickey near a tree.
4 points

Clue 34: Scan the huge mural on the left outdoor wall at the Elds Deer Exhibit for a waving Hidden Mickey in orange flowers.
5 points

Clue 35: Further along the trail, before you get to the aviary entrance, try to spot a classic Mickey in a man's necklace in the carving on the wall.
2 points

★ Before or after an early lunch, wander over to the **Pangani Forest Exploration Trail** in Africa. Look for two Hidden Mickeys in the building with the Naked Mole Rat exhibit.

Clue 36: Find Mickey on a small box.
4 points

Clue 37: Spot a backpack with a Mickey emblem.
3 points

Clue 38: Past the gorilla viewing area, search for a Hidden Jafar.
5 points

★ Eat an early lunch to avoid the crowds. The Rainforest Café at the park entrance is a good place to eat and has an interesting ambiance. Tusker House Restaurant in Africa serves salads and sandwiches.

★ Consult the Times Guide and pick the next convenient shows of *Finding Nemo – The Musical* and *Festival of the Lion King*.

★ See **Finding Nemo – The Musical** at Theater in the Wild in DinoLand.

Clue 39: Look around for a Hidden Mickey near the stage.
3 points

Clue 40: Find two Hidden Mickeys in the show time signs outside.
4 points for spotting both

★ See **Festival of the Lion King** in Camp Minnie-Mickey.

Clue 41: Be alert for a classic Mickey on Timon's float.
4 points

Clue 42: Now search for an upside-down classic Mickey on Timon's float.
4 points

Clue 43: Study the center stage for a classic Mickey.
4 points

Tip: You can (usually) also find these Hidden Mickeys after the show has ended, while the crowd is exiting. (If you need help, ask a Cast Member!)

★ Check other areas in **Camp Minnie-Mickey**.

Clue 44: Spot a rock classic Mickey in a wall near the Greeting Trails.
4 points

★ Now search the camp for a small cabin with classic Mickeys in the woodwork.

Clue 45: You'll find them on both the front and sides of the cabin.
2 points for spotting both

Clue 46: Search the ground near the creek outside the Lion King Theater for a rock classic Mickey.
4 points

Clue 47: Try to find a birdhouse with a Mickey Mouse cutout.
1 point
(Periodically, these birdhouses are moved around to different locations in Camp Minnie-Mickey.)

Clue 48: Find Mickey Mouse's head on top of a nearby flagpole.
4 points

★ Go to Africa and take the Wildlife Express Train to Rafiki's Planet Watch to search **Conservation Station** for a Hidden Mickey bonanza.

Clue 49: Find the Hidden Mickey profile in the changing, repeating panels inside the entrance.
4 points

Clue 50: On the wall mural just to the right, spot a Mickey Mouse profile on an opossum.
4 points

Clue 51: Look for a butterfly wearing classic Mickeys.
3 points

Clue 52: Gaze closely at a spider nearby with a classic Mickey marking.
3 points

Clue 53: Spot a classic Mickey on an ostrich.
3 points

Clue 54: Look for a classic Mickey on a green snake.
3 points

Clue 55: Search for another classic Mickey on a lizard's ear.
4 points

Clue 56: Locate a side-profile Mickey on a hippo.
4 points

Clue 57: Glance at a llama for a classic Mickey.
3 points

Clue 58: A squirrel nearby shows off a classic Mickey.
3 points

Clue 59: Spot a classic Mickey on an alligator.
3 points

Clue 60: Look for a frog with a tiny image of Mickey's face.
5 points

Clue 61: Scan a walrus for a Hidden Mickey.
4 points

Clue 62: Find the Hidden Mickey on an owl.
3 points

Clue 63: Search for the amazing Mickey image on a second butterfly!
5 points

Clue 64: Scan the mural for a fish with a partially hidden classic Mickey.
5 points

Clue 65: Locate a butterfly with two Hidden Mickeys.
4 points

Clue 66: Look around for a frog with a side-profile Mickey.
5 points

Clue 67: Find a yellow butterfly with a classic Mickey.
3 points

 Clue 68: Look lower for a lizard with Mickey spots.
3 points

Clue 69: Scan overhead for a classic Mickey in tree leaves.
3 points

Clue 70: Next to the "Song of the Rainforest" area, spot a fly with a tiny classic Mickey on its back.
5 points

Clue 71: Search for a tiny flower Hidden Mickey at the first entrance to the "Song of the Rainforest" area.
4 points

Clue 72: Look for a classic Mickey indentation on a tree toward the front of the Rainforest area.
3 points

Clue 73: Don't stray far for a Mickey hole in a leaf.
4 points

Clue 74: Check the trees inside the Rainforest area for a side-profile Mickey shadow.
4 points

Clue 75: Look for the classic Mickey shadow on the ceiling near door number eight in the "Song of the Rainforest" area.
4 points

Clue 76: Now find a Hidden Mickey on a tree near door number six.
3 points

Clue 77: Search for a green moss side-profile Mickey in the Rainforest area.
4 points

Clue 78: Walk out to the front of the Rainforest area and search for a side-profile Mickey.
4 points

Clue 79: Spot a classic Mickey made of short plant stalks on the Grandmother Willow tree.
3 points

Clue 80: Also in the Rainforest area, spot a classic Mickey on a cockroach.
4 points

Clue 81: Now find a classic Mickey on a lizard on the same tree.
3 points

Clue 82: Look for a butterfly wearing a tiny Hidden Mickey on this tree.
5 points

Clue 83: Examine the grates around the bottoms of the trees in the main lobby.
2 points

Clue 84: Locate a Hidden Mickey on a plate in a window display at the rear of the lobby.
3 points

Clue 85: Spot a reptile classic Mickey on a ledge in the rear area displays and laboratories.
3 points

★ Walk outside to **Affection Section** to spot another classic Hidden Mickey.

Clue 86: Look closely at the fence on the stage.
3 points

Clue 87: Study the animals in the petting zoo for a Hidden Mickey.
4 points

(Note: These Hidden Mickeys come and go.)

★ Wander on over to the **Wildlife Express Train station** and look for classic Mickeys.

Clue 88: Examine the rafters inside the station.
2 points

★ Ride the train to Africa, then explore the area around the **Harambe Fruit Market** to spot a large Mickey Mouse head in the cement.

Clue 89: Check the beginning of the cement and flagstone path at the side of the Fruit Market.
4 points

Clue 90: Turn left at the opposite end of the path and follow the cement walkway a few feet to find a large, faint classic Mickey in the cement.
5 points

★ Outside the **Mombasa Marketplace store**, look for a classic Mickey formed by a small utility cover and the pebbles adjacent to it.

Clue 91: It's near an entrance door to the store.
5 points

★ Go to the far side of **Tamu Tamu Refreshments**.

Clue 92: Find another classic Mickey formed by a small utility cover and adjacent pebbles.
5 points

Clue 93: Marvel at a Hidden Baloo inside the small seating area behind Tamu Tamu Refreshments.
5 points

Clue 94: Search for another Hidden Character here.
4 points

★ Walk a short way down the **path to Asia**.

Clue 95: Look over to *The Tree of Life* and spot the Hidden Mickey on it. Psst! It's near the hippo.
4 points

★ Cross the bridge to Discovery Island and amble on into **Pizzafari restaurant** to find five Hidden Mickeys.

Clue 96: Spot Mickey in the room across from the food order counters.
3 points

Clue 97: In the first dining room to the left as you walk down the hall, search for a tiny orange classic Mickey.
5 points

Clue 98: In the Nocturnal Room (the dining room directly to the left of the food counters

as you face the counters), study the firefly wings.
3 points

Clue 99: In the Nocturnal Room, look around for a classic Mickey in the trees.
4 points

Clue 100: In the large room past the Nocturnal Room, find some spots on the wall.
3 points

★ Return to DinoLand U.S.A. Enter **The Boneyard** and find three classic Mickeys.

Clue 101: Look under the drinking fountains inside the entrance.
3 points

Clue 102: Walk upstairs. Go to the rear and observe the small classic Mickey in an archeology display.
2 points

Clue 103: Look around the children's dig area for Hidden Mickey hard hats.
2 points

★ Walk to the **Cretaceous Trail** in the middle of DinoLand and go dino hunting.

Clue 104: Find a dark Hidden Mickey on a dinosaur's back.
3 points

★ Go to **TriceraTop Spin**.

Clue 105: Search for a classic Mickey on a dinosaur with a ball in front of the attraction.
3 points

Clue 106: Spot a classic Mickey in one of the parking spaces near the attraction.
3 points

Clue 107: Study the nearby horned dinosaur studded with gems and find a Mickey pin.
4 points

Clue 108: Look around for a Hidden Mickey on a blue dinosaur.
5 points

★ Cross back to **Primeval Whirl** and look for classic Mickeys on the outside of the attraction.

Clue 109: Check the meteors.
5 points for two or more

Clue 110: Watch the parade (usually 4 p.m.) for classic Mickey headlights and a classic Mickey antenna.
3 points for spotting both

★ Walk to the **Creature Comforts shop on Discovery Island** between Pizzafari Restaurant and the bridge to Africa.

Clue 111: Search inside the shop for a black classic Mickey on an animal.
3 points

★ Go Inside the **Island Mercantile shop**.

Clue 112: Spot a classic Mickey on a wall.
5 points

★ Back outside on **Discovery Island**, find a classic Mickey made of green moss.

Clue 113: Study the front of The Tree of Life.
5 points

★ Stroll over to the **Flame Tree Barbecue Restaurant** and find three classic Mickeys.

Clue 114: Search the ground in the food order area for a rock classic Mickey.
4 points

Clue 115: Look at the rear wall of the food order counter area for a classic Mickey.
3 points

Clue 116: Spot a classic Mickey in the seating area outside.
2 points

★ Go to the *Rainforest Café entrance sign* inside the park.

Clue 117: Look for a Hidden Mickey on the sign.
3 points

★ Keep your eyes open *as you leave the park*.

Clue 118: Search the outside walls of the ticket booths for Hidden Mickeys.
4 points for two

Clue 119: Outside the entrance turnstiles, check the metal grates around some of the trees near the tram loading area.
2 points

Now tally your score.

Total Points for
Disney's Animal Kingdom =

How'd you do?
Up to 169 points - Bronze
170 - 338 points - Silver
339 points and over - Gold
424 points - Perfect Score

**Caution:
Don't peek at this
section unless you
really want help!**

Asia

- Expedition Everest

Note: Hints 1 through 10 apply to Hidden Mickeys you'll find only in the Standby queue. Hint 11 is for a Mickey that can be spotted in both the Standby and FASTPASS queues, while Hints 12 and 13 apply to Mickeys that you'll only find in the FASTPASS queue.

Hint 1: The base of a Yeti statue in a sunken courtyard past the first room (an office) has a classic Mickey made of a central circle with swirls for ears.

Hint 2: Just past the first room, classic Mickeys are in the clouds on the left and right sides of a Yeti mural on a wall of a red building.

Hint 3: As you enter the second building, an upside-down classic Mickey is formed by the highest pipes on the top shelf in the right corner.

151

Hint 4: On the far right wall in Tashi's Trek and Tongba Shop, a small Yeti doll in a cupboard on the top right shelf is wearing black Mickey ears.

Hint 5: Also in Tashi's Trek and Tongba Shop, light-switch devices in a glass case on the left side of the queue form a classic Mickey.

Hint 6: Inside the Yeti Museum, a Yeti book is at the far left of the book display, on the right side of the queue after the first left turn. A partial image of Mickey's head and ears is imprinted in the snow on the front cover of the book.

Hint 7: Just past the snow Mickey, a classic Mickey is etched into the top end of a wooden handrail.

Hint 8: Also in the Yeti Museum, dents in a kettle in the second display form a classic Mickey.

Hint 9: The museum also offers a classic Mickey "paw" print. It's at the lower left of a tall glass cabinet display titled "Documenting Bio-Diversity," near the top of the third paper from the left, above the words "Small Mammal Tracks."

Hint 10: The next to last display cabinet in the museum has a photo of a bear with ears that look like Mickey's ears. The bear is on the right side of the cabinet, under the words "The Yeti, Interpreting the Findings."

Hint 11: In the last room before boarding, look for a photo of a woman in blue listening to a hand-held radio. Mickey in his Sorcerer's Hat is etched on a wall to the woman's left.

Hint 12: In the Yeti Museum, a sideways classic Mickey is formed by three dents in a lantern in the second display. You can also spot this lantern image from the Single Rider queue.

Hint 13: In the loading area, look for a classic Mickey in the blue scrollwork above the first window outside.

Hint 14: In the first part of the ride, as your train is climbing the mountain, a dark, melted classic Mickey-shaped spot appears

in the snow to your left. The "ear" farthest away from the train is contiguous with a larger dark spot above it.

Hint 15: Small gold balls form classic Mickeys at the bottom of both sides of a merchandise display in the middle of the gift shop at the ride exit, across from the photo pickup area.

Hint 16: Outside and across from the Serka Zong Bazaar shop, an upside-down classic Mickey is etched near the top of the second stone tablet from the edge closest to the shop.

Hint 17: Outside the attraction, base camp supplies hang in the Gupta's Gear area. A three-circle image hangs among these supplies, near the second post from the end nearest the restrooms.

Africa

- Kilimanjaro Safaris

Hint 18: In elephant country, and about halfway through the ride, the island in the flamingo pond is shaped like a classic Hidden Mickey. It's to the left of the ride vehicle.

Hint 19: The rocks in the lion area are arranged to resemble Donald Duck. Spot his cap first, then his face, eyes, and beak.

DinoLand U.S.A.

- DINOSAUR

Hint 20: Just inside the building entrance, on the right side of the queue, look at the tree at the far left of the painting. There's a classic Mickey on the tree trunk, across from a lower right branch.

Hint 21: Just as the ride starts and before you travel back in time, a classic Mickey at the lower left corner of a white greaseboard appears to the left of your vehicle.

Hint 22: On the mural behind the counter in

the ride's photo-purchase area, a large red dinosaur has a small classic Mickey on its lower neck.

Discovery Island

- It's Tough to be a Bug!

Hint 23: Inside *The Tree of Life*, look for the handicapped entrance doors to *It's Tough to be a Bug!* (You reach them before you get to the main entrance doors to the theater.) Look at the upper left area near the doors to find a small dark classic Mickey.

Asia

- Kali River Rapids

Hint 24: Along the entrance queue, keep your eyes peeled for stone statues in the grass. As you enter the next room, look at the lower left corner of the wall. Three of the plates on the wall above the bicycle form a classic Mickey, tilted down to the right.

- Maharajah Jungle Trek

Hint 25: To the right of the first arch, swirls in the water under a tiger form a classic Mickey.

Hint 26: Inside the first arch, on the left mural, the king's gold earring forms an upside-down classic Mickey.

Hint 27: Inside the first arch, on the left mural, three leaves under the wrist of the king's extended arm form a classic Mickey.

Hint 28: Inside the first arch, on the right mural, a man is wearing an upside-down classic Mickey gold earring.

Hint 29: On the right wall inside the building with arches, two square panels are decorated with flowers. Some of the outer flowers have circles at the bases of their petals that form classic Mickeys.

Hint 30: Inside the second arch, on the left mural, there's a small classic Mickey in a brown rock formation on the left side of the mountains.

Hint 31: Inside the second arch, on the right mural, a classic Mickey appears in the upper part of the left cloud formation.

Hint 32: As you exit the temple ruins, turn to your immediate left to a large wall mural. Among the leaves is a dark green classic Mickey set of leaves. It's about nine feet above the ground and one foot from the bricks at the left side of the mural.

Hint 33: A tree stump shaped rather like a classic Mickey is on the ground to your left (after you exit the temple ruins). It's next to a tree, below a painting of a deer.

Hint 34: In the Elds Deer Exhibit, look left to the huge outdoor wall mural. Mickey is hiding in the right center of the mural, below the third (from the left) of four vertical brick cracks, in some orange flowers and green leaves. He's waving at you!

Hint 35: On a wall to the right, just before you reach the aviary entrance, you'll find an upside-down classic Mickey in the necklace of a man in the middle carving.

Africa

- Pangani Forest Exploration Trail

Hint 36: To the left of the entrance to the building with the Naked Mole Rat Exhibit, a small box of Asepso soap on a shelf behind the desk lamp has a classic Mickey as the "O" in Asepso. You may need to crouch down to spot it.

Hint 37: In the far left corner of the room with the Naked Mole Rat Exhibit, a backpack sports a small classic Mickey emblem on the left side.

Hint 38: A three-dimensional head of Jafar is carved out of a 25- to 30-foot rock. You'll find it past the gorilla viewing area, to the right of the first section of the first suspension bridge.

DinoLand U.S.A.

- Finding Nemo – The Musical

Hint 39: Three bubbles touch to form a classic Mickey at the lower left of the stage.

Hint 40: Two sideways classic Mickeys formed by bubbles are in the outdoor signs announcing the show times for the day. One is in the bottom right corner of the signs, and another is under the 1:00 time disk. These signs are posted on the walkway from Asia and on the walkway from the rest of DinoLand U.S.A.

Camp Minnie-Mickey

- Festival of the Lion King

Hint 41: A white classic Mickey is painted on the lower middle front of Timon's (and the giraffe's) float. You can see it as the float enters the arena.

Hint 42: An upside-down white classic Mickey is on the lower right side of Timon's float, under the giraffe's front leg.

Hint 43: A classic Mickey in relief is on the lower side of the center stage, to the right of some steps and facing the Elephant section of the audience.

– near the last Greeting Trail

Hint 44: A rock classic Mickey is directly across from the entrance to the last Greeting Trail, at the upper part of a short rock wall. One "ear" is light purple.

- cabin on the grounds

Hint 45: Across from the entrance to *Festival of the Lion King*, a cabin housing an ice cream shop has classic Mickeys in the woodwork along the front and sides.

Hint 46: A classic Mickey made of rocks is next to the creek between the Lion King Theater and the small food cabin. It's near the second fence section and between the creek and the food cabin, close to Donald Duck.

156

Hint 47: A birdhouse is often hanging from the front of Chip 'n' Dale's Cookie Cabin. It has a side-profile cutout of Mickey Mouse. Other such birdhouses may be found elsewhere in Camp Minnie-Mickey.

Hint 48: Mickey Mouse's head is on top of the flagpole by the water well, opposite the entrance to the outdoor theater (and before you get to the second bridge to Camp Minnie-Mickey).

Rafiki's Planet Watch

- Conservation Station

Hint 49: The front wall inside the entrance has a section of changing, repeating panels. A small side profile of Mickey Mouse is in the center of the orange starfish.

Hint 50: Find an opossum on the right side of the mural just inside the entrance. There is a side-profile of Mickey Mouse in its eye.

Hint 51: Above the opossum, at the upper right, a butterfly has classic Mickeys on its wings.

Hint 52: About six feet up from the floor, not far from the opossum, a spider has a light pink classic Mickey marking on its thorax.

Hint 53: On the wall to the left of the restrooms, near the entrance, the pupil of an ostrich's eye is a classic Mickey.

Hint 54: Toward the middle of the mural at the front, near the entrance, a green snake sports a black classic Mickey on its upper back.

Hint 55: Near the upper right border of the changing screen, a dark classic Mickey marking is at the top of a green lizard's ear, above a deer.

Hint 56: A hippopotamus is the fifth animal from the left at the bottom of the entrance mural on the left wall. A side-profile Mickey is on its lower jaw, under the middle tooth.

157

Hint 57: To the immediate left of the hippopotamus, a llama sports a dark brown classic Mickey on its neck.

Hint 58: Under the hippopotamus, a squirrel has a black classic Mickey pupil.

Hint 59: On the hippo's right side, an alligator has a small dark classic Mickey to the left of its green eye.

Hint 60: To the right of the alligator, Mickey Mouse's smiling face is under a frog's right eye.

Hint 61: Directly above the frog with the smiling Mickey is a walrus with a dark classic Mickey on the left side (your right) of his neck.

Hint 62: A bit farther along on this left wall mural, the pupils of an owl's eyes are classic Mickeys.

Hint 63: The entrance murals curve toward the inside of the building. On the right curving mural, look for the butterfly with an image of Mickey's face on its body (not its wings!).

Hint 64: Toward the top and near the end of the left side of the entrance mural, a dark classic Mickey, partially hidden by an octopus nearby, is on the side of a fish, to the left of the fish's fin.

Hint 65: Along the bottom of the right mural as you near Rafiki's Theater, two black classic Mickeys are near the bottom of the wings of an orange butterfly under a monkey.

Hint 66: Near the bottom of the same mural, just before the theater, a side-profile Mickey is in a silver frog's left pupil.

Hint 67: Before the first entrance to the "Song of the Rainforest" area, about halfway up the wall and above a bat, a yellow butterfly has a black classic Mickey on its left wing.

Hint 68: In the same area, a tan and green lizard has a group of spots directly behind the eye that form an upside-down classic Mickey.

Hint 69: A hole in the tree leaves overhead resembles a classic Mickey. It's directly above the first entrance.

Hint 70: The fly with a tiny classic Mickey on its back is on the left panel of the first entrance to the "Song of the Rainforest" area.

Hint 71: On the same panel, a tiny yellow flower classic Mickey blooms on a green plant near the floor.

Hint 72: Turn to the right panel at the same entrance to the Rainforest area to see a classic Mickey indentation on a tree. It's about four feet up from the floor.

Hint 73: Look for a classic Mickey hole in a green leaf near the Mickey indentation in Hint 72.

Hint 74: Now go inside to see a side-profile Mickey shadow about seven feet up from the floor on the front of a tree inside the Rainforest area.

Hint 75: Above and in front of door number eight in the Rainforest area, you can spot a dark classic Mickey shadow on the ceiling to the right.

Hint 76: A white classic Mickey is outlined on a tree by door number six, to the left of the words "The Accidental Florist."

Hint 77: Turn around and walk out toward the lobby to look at the right side of the tree with "The Song of the Rainforest" sign (the Grandmother Willow tree). A rear horizontal panel has a green moss side-profile Mickey about six feet up from the floor.

Hint 78: A side-profile Mickey indentation appears on the same tree under the sign and to the lower right (as you face her) of Grandmother Willow's face. (Tip: You have to walk further into the lobby to spot it.)

Hint 79: Three plant stalks form a classic Mickey in the mural near the floor on the bottom left of the Grandmother Willow tree, as you face it from the lobby.

Hint 80: To the right of the Grandmother Willow tree, there is a cockroach display inside a tree in front of the "Song of the Rainforest" area. A cockroach inside and toward the back of the tree bears a dark classic Mickey on its back.

Hint 81: A lizard above the "Giant Cockroach" sign on the same tree has a classic Mickey above its front leg.

Hint 82: On the left front of the tree with the cockroach display, a light brown butterfly about six and a half feet up from the floor has a tiny black classic Mickey on its back between the wings.

Hint 83: The grates around the bottoms of the trees in the lobby have classic Mickey patterns, as do those outside by Affection Section.

Hint 84: A classic Mickey on a "Microtiter Plate" is usually in the first display room to the right in the rear of the lobby, in the second window of the "Wildlife Tracking Center." The plate changes color from time to time!

Hint 85: A classic Mickey made of three containers with reptile skins is on a ledge in the far left window of a room with reptiles.

- Affection Section

Hint 86: By the animal petting area, look for an orange classic Mickey on a blue background on a wooden panel at the rear of the stage. It's next to the shelf and to the right of the door with lizards.

Hint 87: One of the animals usually has a classic Mickey shaved on its coat.

- Wildlife Express Train station

Hint 88: High up in the rafters inside the train station, look for classic Mickeys where the beams intersect.

Africa

- in and around Harambe

Hint 89: At one side of the Harambe Fruit Market, a short cement and flagstone path with benches leads through some trees. A large Mickey Mouse head in the cement marks the beginning of the path. It's several feet in diameter.

Hint 90: At the opposite end of this short path, turn left onto the cement walkway and walk a few feet. Nearby you'll find a faint depression in the cement that forms a very large classic Mickey (six feet or more in diameter). This HM is best seen after a rain when the pavement is wet. It is often partially covered with parked strollers.

Hint 91: Outside, near an entrance door to the Mombasa Marketplace store, you'll find a classic Mickey formed by a small utility cover (with the letter "D" in the middle) and the pebbles adjacent to it. The cover is on the path on the side facing the Tusker House Restaurant.

Hint 92: Near Tamu Tamu Refreshments, on the walkway that connects Africa and Asia, a small utility cover and the pebbles adjacent to it form a similar classic Mickey. Here, the utility cover has the letter "S" in the middle.

Hint 93: Inside the small seating area behind Tamu Tamu Refreshments, a white Hidden Baloo is on the wall nearest the path to Asia. He's often covered by a curtain.

Hint 94: Inside the small seating area behind Tamu Tamu Refreshments, a Hidden Scar (the lion) is on a corner wall and under vases that are in recessed openings.

Hint 95: On the back of *The Tree of Life*, and visible from the path between Africa and Asia, is an upside-down classic Mickey. Look above the eye of the hippopotamus to spot him.

Discovery Island

- Pizzafari restaurant

Hint 96: A yellow classic Mickey image is under a bat, which is on a wall in the seating area across from the food order counters. As you enter the room, turn left to face the rear wall and look for the bat on the right.

Hint 97: On the rear wall of the first dining room to the left as you walk down the hall away from the food order area, a tiny orange classic Mickey is at the lower left of a turtle shell.

Hint 98: On the left rear wall of the Nocturnal Room (the dining room directly to the left of the food counters as you face the counters), the wings of the lower left firefly resemble Mickey Mouse ears.

Hint 99: In the same room, a classic Mickey made of tree leaves lies near a reddish raccoon. It's tilted with the "ears" to the left as you face the wall.

Hint 100: In the large room just past the Nocturnal Room, a gray spot with two white ears on the far wall forms a classic Mickey in the tree branches to the right of the leopard.

DinoLand U.S.A.

- The Boneyard

Hint 101: Just inside the entrance, you'll find a reddish-brown classic Mickey pattern in the flooring under the drinking fountains.

Hint 102: Upstairs to the rear left, in a fenced off archeology display, three coins on a table form a classic Mickey.

Hint 103: On the right side of the children's dig area, in a small display, a fan and two hard hats form a classic Mickey.

- Cretaceous Trail

Hint 104: At one end of this short trail in the middle of DinoLand, you'll find a large di-

nosaur. Three dark spots on its middle back form a classic Mickey.

- TriceraTop Spin

Hint 105: In front of *TriceraTop Spin*, a green dinosaur balances a red and yellow striped ball on its horns. A classic Mickey is formed in the scales on the dino's right side, under the front horn.

Hint 106: In the parking spaces across from *TriceraTop Spin*, a classic Mickey can be found in the cement at the front of the second parking space from the horned dinosaur.

Hint 107: On the right side of the horned dinosaur (as you face it), a gold "Steamboat Willie" Cast Member pin is located on a spine on the dinosaur's upper back, near a large silver medallion.

Hint 108: A dark blue classic Mickey is near the left wrist of the blue dinosaur holding the "Chester & Hester's Dino-Rama" sign near *TriceraTop Spin*.

- Primeval Whirl

Hint 109: In the outside decorations, the sides of several meteors sport classic Mickey craters. One is under "Head for the Hills," one is over the "Primeval Whirl" sign, and a third is on the right side of the attraction near a dinosaur holding a sign.

Hint 110: The parade (usually at 4:00 p.m.) abounds in classic and décor Mickeys. The first jeep has classic Mickey headlights and the last vehicle has classic Mickey antenna dishes on the flagpole.

Discovery Island

- Creature Comforts Shop

Hint 111: A black classic Mickey is on the lower right part of a beetle, which is on a merchandise stand inside the store. If you face the outside windows of the store, the beetle is to the left of the large giraffe.

- Island Mercantile Shop

Hint 112: A classic Mickey made of spots is on a lower cell of an orange and blue bumblebee honeycomb on an inside post. It's on the rear wall opposite the entrance doors closest to the walkway to The Oasis.

- The Tree of Life

Hint 113: On the front of *The Tree of Life*, facing The Oasis and about one-third the distance up the trunk from the bottom, is a classic Mickey made of green moss. You'll find it to the left of the buffalo.

- Flame Tree Barbecue Restaurant

Hint 114: In the food order area, rocks embedded in the ground form a classic Mickey at the front edge of the rock border and next to the third post from the right.

Hint 115: Two rhinos are on the right wall inside the far right food service window. A classic Mickey is on the rear of the second rhino, which is next to the back wall. Three circles in the lower middle of the dark blue area approximate a classic Mickey.

Hint 116: At the outside seating area behind the food order counters, grates on the ground near trees have classic Mickey circles. Find them near the first set of tables to the right, where there is a statue of a frog holding up a pig. These grates can also be found in other nearby areas.

- Rainforest Café

Hint 117: A green lizard at the Rainforest Café entrance sign that is inside the park has an upside-down classic Mickey in the middle of the circles on its neck.

Outside the entrance turnstiles
to the park

Hint 118: When you head out of the park, turn back as you pass the ticket booths. You'll find two rock classic Mickeys, one on the right-hand corner of the wall of the rightmost ticket booth and the other in the wall of the leftmost ticket booth near the ground, toward the front of the booth's left side.

Hint 119: Outside the entrance turnstiles, near the tram loading area, the metal grates at the bases of some of the trees incorporate classic Mickeys in their design.

Notes

Resort Hotel Scavenger Hunt

• • • • • • • • • • • • • • • • • • •

Walt Disney World's resort hotels are filled with Mickeys, hidden and otherwise. The majority are what I like to call décor Hidden Mickeys, imaginative decorations that vary among the hotels and change periodically over time. Such Hidden Mickeys can be found along hotel hallways in the carpet, wallpaper, and lampshades. They appear in the guest rooms on covers for drinking glasses, bedspreads, pillows, day beds, furniture, lamps, lamp shades, room curtains, shower curtains, wall pictures, wallpaper, carpets, soap, the outer wrapping of toilet paper rolls, and other items. Guest laundry rooms sometimes have Hidden Mickeys on the soap vending machines and in the bubbles on wall paintings, and resort laundry bins and carts show off classic and side-profile Mickeys. Mickey Mouse imprints can often be found in the sand in hotel ashtrays.

In the restaurants, pancakes, waffles, butter pats, pasta, pizza, pepperoni on the pizza, and the arrangement of dishes and condiments, among other items, are sometimes Mickey-shaped. Mugs, paper plates, and other items in the gift shops can sport hiding Mickeys. Even the utilities embrace Mickey. Manhole covers and survey markers throughout Walt Disney World often have classic Mickey designs in the center.

Generally, I do not include such décor Mickeys in the scavenger hunts unless they are truly unique (as many of the carpet Mickeys are) and are easily accessible to Hidden Mickey hunters at the hotels and other WDW areas. So don't be surprised to discover dozens of Mickeys at the hotels you visit that aren't included in this scavenger hunt. They're fun to spot but you don't get points for finding them.

The best way to hunt for Hidden Mickeys at the hotels is by car. However, buses to all the WDW hotels are available from Downtown Disney (the major bus depot is at the

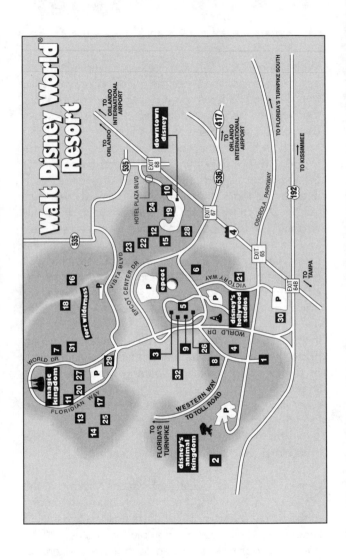

18 Pioneer Hall
19 Pleasure Island, in Downtown Disney
20 Polynesian
21 Pop Century
22 Port Orleans – French Quarter
23 Port Orleans – Riverside
24 Saratoga Springs
25 Shades of Green
26 Swan
27 Transportation and Ticket Center
28 Typhoon Lagoon
29 WDW Speedway
30 Wide World of Sports
31 Wilderness Lodge
32 Yacht Club
P Parking

1 All-Star Resorts
2 Animal Kingdom Lodge
3 Beach Club
4 Blizzard Beach
5 BoardWalk
6 Caribbean Beach
7 Contemporary
8 Coronado Springs
9 Dolphin
10 Downtown Disney
11 Grand Floridian
12 Lake Buena Vista Golf Course
13 Magnolia Golf Course
14 Oak Trails Golf Course
15 Old Key West
16 Osprey Ridge Golf Course
17 Palm Golf Course

far end of the Marketplace). If you choose to bus around, be prepared for leisurely hunting. You won't be able to visit as many hotels in a given time frame as you would with a car.

Of course, driving means parking, and it's not always a slam-dunk. Guard gates stand watch at most WDW hotels. When you drive up, tell the guard that you're a Hidden Mickey freak and want to look for Hidden Mickeys at the hotel. You'll generally be greeted with a smile, an opened gate, and a wave — along with a "Good luck!" or "Go freak out!" to encourage you on your quest. In the event you aren't allowed to park, drive on to another hotel on the scavenger hunt and take transportation (bus, boat or monorail) to the one you want to explore. If you're really lucky, you may have a spouse, friend or family member who is willing to drop you off and pick you up.

Again, be considerate of other guests and Cast Members. Ask permission to look around restaurants and avoid searching for Hidden Mickeys at meal times unless you are one of the diners. Even then be careful to stay out of the way — especially of waiters with full trays. Let others share in the fun by telling them what you are up to if they notice you looking around.

Two important notes:
• I've arranged this hunt in a logical, efficient progression that I imagine you could follow in a car. However, you may want to hunt just one hotel or group of sister hotels at a time. That's why I list the perfect score for each resort hotel (and hotel group) in parentheses after the hotel (or group) name in the Clues section.

• This scavenger hunt includes only those WDW resorts in which I found Hidden Mickeys. If I found no convincing (to me) Hidden Mickeys in a hotel, I didn't include it in the hunt. Keep your eyes open; you may spot a Hidden Mickey that I haven't found (yet).

I'll start with the Animal Kingdom Lodge Resort, but you can start (and stop) wherever you want. Have fun!

Animal Kingdom Lodge Resort
(111 points)

Clue 1: Walk toward the "E1" parking lot sign from the AKL entrance. Search the pavement for a classic Mickey. (This Mickey is hard to find!)
5 points

Clue 2: Look up for a classic Mickey outside near the hotel's main entrance.
2 points

Clue 3: Find a classic Mickey on a wall mural between the outer and inner entrance doors to the main lobby.
2 points

Clue 4: Inside the main lobby, spot a classic Mickey on a chandelier.
3 points

Clue 5: Check the logs banded to wood supports around the main lobby. Find any classic Mickeys?
2 points

Clue 6: Look for a classic Mickey on the rock formation next to the short bridge on the right side of the main lobby (as you face it on entering).
4 points

Clue 7: Search the Kudu Trail at the rear of the lobby for a classic Mickey on a post.
4 points

Clue 8: Study the first observation patio along the Kudu Trail for yet another classic Mickey.
5 points

Clue 9: Try to spot a green Hidden Mickey in side profile outside the rear doors of the main lobby. He's on the vine-covered column, on your right as you exit, and he's looking into the lobby.
5 points

Clue 10: On the trail to Arusha Rock Overlook, outside the rear exit from the main lobby, explore the decorative reliefs on the

rock wall for a giraffe with a classic Mickey.
3 points

Clue 11: Spot another classic Mickey along the walk-way in Arusha Rock Overlook.
4 points

Clue 12: Study the rock wall at the rear of Arusha Rock Overlook for a classic Mickey.
5 points

Clue 13: Search for a classic Mickey on the rock wall as you descend the stairs from the right side of the main lobby to Boma restaurant.
4 points

Clue 14: Examine the chairs inside Boma restaurant.
2 points

Clue 15: Inside Jiko restaurant, check out the ceiling above the large oven exhausts.
2 points

Clue 16: From inside Jiko restaurant, spot a classic Mickey out the window.
5 points

Clue 17: From the path alongside the walkway to the pool's water slide, find a classic Mickey impression low on a rock.
4 points

Clue 18: Further along this walkway, around the back of the swimming pool, look for a light-colored classic Mickey cut into the rock wall.
4 points

Clue 19: From a fence at the flamingo overlook, study the rock wall for a classic Mickey.
4 points

Clue 20: Search the wall outside in the back of The Mara eatery seating area for a classic Mickey.

4 points

★ Now find three classic Mickeys inside **The Mara food area**.

Clue 21: One is on the left upper wall.
3 points

Clue 22: Another is above the bakery.
3 points

Clue 23: The third is on the right upper wall.
3 points

Clue 24: Spot a classic Mickey in the elevator to the Fitness Center.
2 points

Clue 25: Walk around to spot some classic Mickeys in the carpet below the 5th floor as well as either on or above the 5th floor.
4 points for two or more

★ Walk to **Kidani Village**. (23 points)

Clue 26: Look for Mickey on a clock.
4 points

Clue 27: Search high for Mickey in the lobby.
5 points

Clue 28: Spot him as you approach Sanaa restaurant.
4 points

Clue 29: Locate Mickey on a wall inside Sanaa.
3 points

Clue 30: Study Sanaa's dining tables for Mickey.
3 points

Clue 31: Now leave the restaurant and find Mickey on a rock outside.
4 points

Disney's All-Star Resorts
(16 points)

★ **All-Star Sports Resort** (10 points)

Clue 32: Go to the main building gift shop and find classic Mickeys in the carpet.
2 points

Clue 33: Study the gift shop walls for Hidden Mickeys.
3 points for two or more

Clue 34: Walk around the food court for a Hidden Mickey on the wall.
3 points

Clue 35: Find the classic Mickey in the cement outdoors behind and to the right of the registration building. Psst! He's near the Mickey Mouse statue.
2 points

★ *All-Star Music Resort* (5 points)

Clue 36: Examine the Jazz Inn courtyard to spot classic Mickey ears.
3 points

Clue 37: Take a look at the boots in the Country Fair area.
2 points

★ *All-Star Movies Resort* (1 point)

Clue 38: Check out Andy's Room in the resort's "Toy Story" section.
1 point

Coronado Springs Resort
(26 points)

Clue 39: Take a good look at the large wooden doors at the front entrance to the main lobby.
3 points

Clue 40: Now study the wooden doors at the exit labeled El Centro.
3 points

Clue 41: Walk to the hallway outside the Veracruz Exhibit Hall in the Convention Center and look around for two classic Mickeys.
4 points for spotting both

Clue 42: Examine the cement near the Marina rental gazebo.
4 points

Clue 43: Spot a classic Mickey at the Dig Site swimming pool on a wall facing the lake.
3 points

Clue 44: Now find a classic Mickey on a wall facing the Dig Site pool.
3 points

Clue 45: Look for a whitish classic Mickey on a stone block on the Mayan pyramid at the Dig Site.
4 points

Clue 46: Check the bus stop signs around the periphery of the resort.
2 points for one or more

Pop Century Resort
(35 points)

Clue 47: Search for a fish bowl with a Hidden Mickey near the check-in area.
4 points

Clue 48: Look high for a Hidden Mickey in the Everything Pop Food Court.
3 points

Clue 49: Look low for Hidden Mickeys at the Everything Pop Food Court.
3 points for two or more

Clue 50: Locate two Hidden Mickeys (one purple and one green) on walls in the food court.
4 points for spotting both

Clue 51: In the shop adjoining the Everything Pop Food Court, find Hidden Mickeys on merchandise stands.
2 points

Clue 52: Spot a classic Mickey on a wall near the Computer Pool.
4 points

Clue 53: Marvel at a Hidden Mickey on a wall behind Mowgli on the '60s building.
5 points

Clue 54: Notice a Hidden Mickey in the laundry room near the Hippy Dippy Pool.
4 points

Clue 55: Find Hidden Mickeys in a laundry room near the Bowling Pool.
3 points for two Hidden Mickeys

Clue 56: Look around for a Hidden Mickey near the bus stop out front of the Pop Century lobby.
3 points

Caribbean Beach Resort
(15 points)

Clue 57: Spot a classic Mickey on the lighthouse behind Old Port Royale.
2 points

Clue 58: Search for a classic Mickey in the children's water play area near the main pool.
4 points

Clue 59: Study the rockwork of the main pool for a classic Mickey.
5 points

Clue 60: In Shutters restaurant, find a classic Mickey in a painting.
4 points

Downtown Disney Area Resorts
(86 points)

★ *Old Key West Resort* (23 points)

Clue 61: Check the fences in Conch Flats General Store.
2 points

Clue 62: Take a close look at the fence railings in the registration area.
2 points

Clue 63: At the pool, spot a Mickey with a big mouth.
3 points

Clue 64: Find a Hidden Mickey near the steps to the water slide.
4 points

Clue 65: Notice the design of certain railings on the guest buildings outside.
2 points

★ Search for classic Mickeys formed by three shell imprints in the cement on the paths leading from parking spaces to Building 36.

Clue 66: Search the cement on the right side of the first path for imprints.
5 points

Clue 67: On the second path, explore the corner of the sidewalk after the first right turn.
5 points

(More of these amazing Mickeys may be scattered around Old Key West Resort.)

★ *Port Orleans Resort – French Quarter*
(5 points)

Clue 68: Find a classic Mickey in the registration area.
3 points

Clue 69: Look up for a classic Mickey in the food court area.
2 points

★ *Port Orleans Resort – Riverside* (14 points)

Clue 70: Look for classic Mickeys in the latticework of the registration area.
2 points

Clue 71: Also in the registration area, find more classic Mickeys near the giant fans.
2 points

Clue 72: Now spot Hidden Mickeys on the fans themselves.
3 points

Clue 73: Search for Mickey in a building to the right of Oak Manor.
3 points

Clue 74: Find Mickeys at Parterre Place.
4 points

★ *Saratoga Springs Resort* (44 points)

Clue 75: Behind the Artist's Palette shop, look around for Mickey on a door handle.
5 points

Clue 76: Notice classic Mickeys on a jacket near The Turf Club.
2 points

Clue 77: Find more Mickey images inside on a wall.
2 points for one or more

Clue 78: Check out a statue outside the main lobby for three pairs of Hidden Mickeys.
(Note: The statue also sports a décor Mickey.)
10 points for finding all six

Clue 79: Search for two Hidden Mickeys near stairs outside the Artist's Palette.
5 points for spotting both

Clue 80: Look for Hidden Mickeys on the outside wall and the downstairs entrance door of the spa.
4 points for spotting both

Clue 81: Admire the guest buildings for small Mickeys.
2 points

Clue 82: Search for a Hidden Mickey on an outdoor wall, near the check-in point.
5 points

Clue 83: Look around for Hidden Mickeys on outdoor wall lights.
4 points

178

Clue 84: Find classic Mickeys in the Villa courtyards.
2 points

Clue 85: Locate Mickey near the Grandstand Pool.
3 points

Epcot Resorts
(99 points)

To explore the following hotels, park at one and walk around Crescent Lake to the others. Smile and tell the guards that you're searching for Hidden Mickeys.

★ *BoardWalk Resort* (32 points)

Clue 86: Spot two classic Mickeys on a horse in the main lobby.
3 points

Clue 87: Search for a classic Mickey on the lobby wall.
4 points

Clue 88: Find classic Mickeys on lamps in the lobby.
2 points for one or more

Clue 89: Wander around the guest room and elevator hallways in the BoardWalk Inn and Villas.
10 points for five or more different Mickeys; 4 more points for a Tinker Bell!

Clue 90: Pick out at least five character images near the elevators on the BoardWalk Villas' lobby floor.
5 points for finding all five

Clue 91: Look around for a Hidden Mickey near Seashore Sweets.
4 points

★ *Beach Club Resort* (45 points)

Clue 92: Search for Mickey Mouse along the inside walkway in front of the Cape May Café.
3 points

★ Walk to the Beach Club Solarium to find more Hidden Mickeys. Psst! Check the walls.

Clue 93: Spot some car tires with Mickey's full face.
3 points

Clue 94: Now look for classic Mickeys in the same general area.
2 points

Clue 95: Gaze at Mickey's face in the sky.
3 points

Clue 96: Search for Mickey on the sand.
4 points

Clue 97: Then find classic Mickeys in the water.
2 points

Clue 98: Do you see other classic Mickeys floating in the air?
2 points

Clue 99: Squint for a Hidden Mickey atop a building.
5 points

Clue 100: Walk to a guest room hallway to find classic Mickeys under your feet.
2 points for one or more

Clue 101: Now stare at the hallway walls for Mickey images.
3 points

Clue 102: Look down near the Beach Club lobby elevators for two classic Mickeys.
3 points for spotting both

Clue 103: Find Mickey in the Marketplace shop.
2 points

Clue 104: Study the area near the entrance to the Beach Club Villas for a classic Mickey.
4 points

Clue 105: Search at the entrance to Cape May Café for a Hidden Mickey.
3 points

Clue 106: Wander into the Beaches & Cream Soda Shop for a tasty Hidden Mickey on the wall.
4 points

★ *Yacht Club Resort* (22 points)

Clue 107: Study the globe in the main lobby.
5 points

Clue 108: Look for a cabinet in the main lobby with character names on the drawers.
4 points

Clue 109: Check out the lobby carpet.
2 points

Clue 110: Go up to the fourth floor to spot a Hidden Mickey near the elevators.
2 points

Clue 111: Check out other resort carpets for Mickeys.
4 points for two or more

Clue 112: In the Yachtsman Steakhouse, look for the photograph of (now deceased) Minnie Moo, a cow born with a black classic Mickey on her side. (You may have to ask a Cast Member where the photo is located. It's sometimes not on public display.)
5 points

Fort Wilderness Resort
(11 points)

Clue 113: Search the Horse Barn for a Hidden Mickey.
5 points

Clue 114: Visit the Blacksmith (near the Horse Barn) and find a Hidden Mickey.
3 points

Clue 115: Go to the Kennel building near the front parking area to find Hidden Mickeys.
3 points

Wilderness Lodge Resort
(97 points)

Clue 116: Check out the signs on the right side of the entrance drive.
2 points

Clue 117: Search out a classic on the guard-gate kiosk.
3 points

Clue 118: Near the car unloading area, look up for a classic Mickey etched in a support pole above a black metal band.
4 points

Clue 119: Search for a classic Mickey etched in another support pole and partially hidden under a black metal band.
4 points

Clue 120: Glance down for a tiny classic Mickey traced in the cement on a black stripe.
5 points

Clue 121: Look up again for a classic Mickey etched on a side support pole.
4 points

Clue 122: Find a classic Mickey on a large key in the registration area.
1 point

Clue 123: Look for Mickey driving a bus overhead.
2 points

Clue 124: Find a classic Mickey on the rock of the main lobby fireplace.
5 points

Clue 125: Peek at a fireplace inside the Whispering Canyon Café for a classic Mickey. (Ask a Cast Member to let you into the rear of the café.)
4 points

Clue 126: Look for a classic Mickey on a wall map at the entrance stairs to the Territory Lounge.
3 points

Clue 127: Now go inside and spot a classic Mickey on a ceiling mural above the bar.
4 points

182

Clue 128: Inside the Artist Point restaurant, spot a classic Mickey in a large mural above

the entrance to the rear left dining area.
4 points

Clue 129: Now scan the walls of the restaurant for Winnie the Pooh.
3 points

Clue 130: Search inside the Roaring Fork snack bar for a Hidden Mickey in a display case.
3 points

Clue 131: Find a classic Mickey in one or more lights near the elevators close to the snack bar.
3 points

Clue 132: Glance at the hallway walls for small Hidden Mickeys.
3 points

Clue 133: Look down in the hallways for more.
2 points

Clue 134: Locate a classic Mickey near Room 6100.
3 points

Clue 135: Explore one floor down for a classic Mickey near Room 5066.
3 points

Clue 136: Find another classic near Room 4035.
3 points

Clue 137: Search for a classic Mickey in the rock outside at Fire Rock Geyser.
4 points

Clue 138: Find stairs outside an exit door from the main building (on the side toward the Boat and Bike Rental) and look up for a classic Mickey.
4 points

★ *in the Cub's Den* (21 points)

Tip: Visit in the afternoon if possible. It's less crowded then, and the Cast Members are more likely to let you in. Tell them you're searching for Hidden Mickeys.

Clue 139: Spot a plush Mickey doll in a mural.
2 points

Clue 140: Look higher for a side-profile Mickey.
3 points

Clue 141: Find a classic Mickey in the same mural.
3 points

Clue 142: Search for three classic Mickeys on a wall near the Wilderness Lodge Villas' lobby.
4 points for finding all three

Clue 143: Smile back at Mickey hiding in a hole in a beam in the lobby.
5 points

Clue 144: Locate a side profile of Mickey on a wall near the lobby.
4 points

Magic Kingdom Monorail Resorts
(111 points)

To find the Hidden Mickeys in these resorts and the nearby Wedding Pavilion, park at the Polynesian or the Grand Floridian and ride the monorail to the other two resorts and past the Wedding Pavilion. Or if you prefer, walk or drive to the Wedding Pavilion. Note: The Polynesian has the bigger parking lot.

★ *Polynesian Resort* (39 points)

Clue 145: On the lower level, look for a classic Mickey on the floor near the waterfall.
4 points

Clue 146: Spot three Hidden Mickeys in the Tiki Boutique store.
4 points for finding all three

Clue 147: Search for another just outside the store.
3 points

Clue 148: Check the carpet nearby for classic Mickeys.
3 points for three or more

Clue 149: Study the bamboo-ring wall decorations by the corner staircase.
3 points

★ Find two Hidden Mickeys in Trader Jack's gift shop.

Clue 150: Look on top of the merchandise cabinets in front of the upper wall mural.
1 point

Clue 151: Now check out the chair.
2 points

Clue 152: Study the nearby carpet.
4 points for two classic Mickeys

Clue 153: At the Kona Island coffee bar, search for a small classic Mickey.
5 points

Clue 154: Look around inside Captain Cook's snack bar for a Hidden Mickey that comes and goes.
5 points

Clue 155: Study the sign for Moana Mickey's Arcade.
2 points

Clue 156: Look down for Hidden Mickeys in hallways and elevators.
3 points for spotting both

★ *Wedding Pavilion* (3 points)

Note: A Hidden Mickey may be lurking inside, but the building isn't open to the general public.

Clue 157: As your monorail car passes by the pavilion buildings, observe the weather vane.
3 points

★ *Grand Floridian Resort* (27 points)

The Hidden Mickeys here are all classics.

Clue 158: Take a good look at the weather vanes on the roofs.
3 points for one or more

Clue 159: Check the large trolley carts outside the hotel.
1 point

Clue 160: Look near 1900 Park Fare restaurant.
3 points

Clue 161: Study the lobby carpet.
2 points

Clue 162: Search for Mickeys on the lobby staircase.
2 points

Clue 163: Spot Mickey on the outside of the ornate lobby elevator by the stairs.
4 points

Clue 164: Find Hidden Mickeys in the hallway walls.
2 points for one or more

Clue 165: Now look down for others in the hallways.
2 points

Clue 166: Locate two classic Mickeys inside Gasparilla Grill & Games.
4 points for spotting both

Clue 167: Find Mickey and other characters in the lobbies of the outer buildings.
4 points for four or more

★ *Contemporary Resort* (42 points)

Clue 168: From the window of the California Grill restaurant, on the top floor, spot a stretched out Mickey watchband on the ground in front of the hotel.
4 points

Clue 169: Check out the (closed) glass doors of the back room inside the California Grill restaurant. (If the doors are open, you may not see the Hidden Mickey.)
4 points

Clue 170: Go to the sixth floor and walk in the direction of the Transportation and Ticket Center to an outside balcony to spot this amazing Hidden Mickey.
5 points

186

Clue 171: Look for Mickey's profile inside Chef Mickey's restaurant.
1 point

Clue 172: Check out some classic Mickeys on a shelf inside Chef Mickey's.
2 points

Clue 173: Don't miss Mickey's ears at the rear of Chef Mickey's!
3 points

Clue 174: Find Mickey on a wall near Contempo Café.
3 points

Clue 175: Look high for a classic Mickey on an animal.
4 points

Clue 176: Search for a stick-figure Mickey near the shops.
3 points

Clue 177: Look for Mickey in The Game Station Arcade.
3 points

Clue 178: Find a classic Mickey silhouette in the bricks behind the main hotel. Psst! It's near Mickey Mouse himself.
2 points

Clue 179: Locate a Hidden Mickey in The Sand Bar.
3 points

Clue 180: Spot Mickey in the tile at the exit from the Garden Building to the parking lot.
5 points

Shades of Green Resort
(9 points)

Clue 181: Search for four classic Mickeys in the lobby.
5 points for finding all four

Clue 182: Find a large classic Mickey outside (or on a map of the resort).
4 points

187

Total Points for Hotel Hunt =

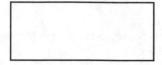

How'd you do?

A perfect score for this scavenger hunt is 616. But here is a breakdown by resort and resort group, so that you compare your score with the perfect score for the areas you've covered. You'll find the total points for each section in parentheses. Give yourself gold if you score at least 80% of the points available. Bronze for at least 40%.

Animal Kingdom Lodge Resort (111)
Disney's All-Star Resorts (16)
   All-Star Sports Resort (10)
   All-Star Music Resort (5)
   All-Star Movies Resort (1)
Coronado Springs Resort (26)
Pop Century Resort (35)
Caribbean Beach Resort (15)
Downtown Disney Area Resorts (86)
   Old Key West Resort (23)
   Port Orleans Resort – French Quarter (5)
   Port Orleans Resort – Riverside (14)
   Saratoga Springs Resort (44)
Epcot Resorts (99)
   BoardWalk Resort (32)
   Beach Club Resort (45)
   Yacht Club Resort (22)
Fort Wilderness Resort (11)
Wilderness Lodge Resort (97)
Magic Kingdom Monorail Resorts (111)
   Polynesian Resort (39)
   Wedding Pavilion (3)
   Grand Floridian Resort (27)
   Contemporary Resort (42)
Shades of Green (9)

Caution:
Don't peek at this section unless you really want help!

Animal Kingdom Lodge Resort

Hint 1: A small classic Mickey tar spot is in the parking lot of the Animal Kingdom Lodge. Walk straight ahead from the circle drive exit from the car unloading area at the AKL entrance. About 45 feet before the "E1" sign, search the pavement in front of the second grass island (counting from the main parking lot crossroad).

Hint 2: Outside, above the lower roof, the second tall figure to the left of the car baggage drop-off area has a classic Mickey in his mouth.

Hint 3: On the right wall mural between the outer and inner entrance doors to the main lobby, an orange and brown creature sports a classic Mickey in a circle on its mid back.

Hint 4: Inside the main lobby, you can find a classic Mickey near the bottom of the second chandelier on the right (as you face in from the front entrance). The Hidden Mickey is near the bottom of one of the shields.

189

Hint 5: Around the main lobby, classic Mickeys are formed by logs banded to wood supports. One of the best is the second support on the right (as you enter the lobby from the front doors). It's on the second level, on the side away from the main lobby entrance.

Hint 6: On the right side of the main lobby (as you face in from the front entrance), a short bridge crosses a rockbound pool of water. A classic Mickey is visible on the rock from the side of the bridge nearest the lobby. It's toward the rear on the right side. To spot it, look for the first recess in the rock from the right edge of the pool. Mickey is at the back of this recess, above the water line.

Hint 7: From the main lobby, go down the staircase at the rear of the lobby. Turn left and walk down the Kudu Trail hallway. In the first small lobby, a classic Mickey is on the top end of a post nearest the elevator, above the second rope binding and near the ceiling.

Hint 8: On the first observation patio along the Kudu Trail, a classic Mickey is etched on an arm of one of the rocking chairs.

Hint 9: Outside the rear doors of the main lobby, a green Mickey in side profile hides in the decorative vines to the right as you exit. He is about two-thirds of the way up the side of the vine-covered column, above the middle horizontal brace. Look for him at the top of an open space in the vines. He's looking into the lobby.

Hint 10: Outside the rear exit from the main lobby, on the left side of the trail to Arusha Rock Overlook, check the rock wall for a decorative relief of a group of giraffes. You'll find a classic Mickey among the spots on the middle of the large giraffe in the center, above the inner front leg.

Hint 11: Along the walkway in Arusha Rock Overlook, a rock sports a classic Mickey. Look for it where the trail first turns left between rock walls. It's on the right side in the first small alcove, about six feet up from the path and under a large overhanging rock.

Hint 12: At the very back of Arusha Rock Overlook is a tiny, salmon-colored classic Mickey. It's in the right middle of the rock wall opposite the Animal Overlook sign and behind the Cast Member's umbrella, about 5½ feet above the ground to the right of a vertical crack in the rock.

Hint 13: Toward the bottom of the staircase that winds from the right side of the main lobby to Boma restaurant, there's a classic Mickey on the rock wall next to a waterfall.

Hint 14: Inside Boma, you'll see classic Mickeys on some of the chairs with tall metal backs.

Hint 15: Inside Jiko restaurant, a classic Mickey is formed on the ceiling above the two large orange oven exhausts and the white column behind them.

Hint 16: Enter Jiko and walk to the third table on your left, next to the glass windows. Outside in the shallow pool area, a classic Mickey is sculpted on the first rock island from the left that has a pillar jutting out of it.

Hint 17: Outside the exit from the restaurants, a large rock on the left side of the path behind the water slide has a classic Mickey impressed on its lower half near the ground. The rock is about three-quarters of the way along the walkway to the water slide. A small light pole juts out of the top of this rock.

Hint 18: A light-colored classic Mickey is cut into a rock wall behind the swimming pool. The wall forms the back of the pool's water slide. The Mickey is several feet above the walkway, below a gazebo that marks the starting point for the water slide.

Hint 19: Walk behind the pool to the bird and flamingo overlook. From the rightmost Bird Spotter Guide on the fence along the main trail, look to your right to the opposite fence. About two-thirds of the distance along this fence from the main trail, a pinkish classic

Mickey with a white right ear is about one foot down from the top of the rock.

Hint 20: A classic stone Mickey is on the rear of the short wall behind The Mara seating area. It's about three feet up from the ground, behind an emergency phone and a tall brown pole.

Hint 21: In the food area of The Mara, a classic Mickey is on the upper left wall in the third leaf from the left tree (in the mural of falling leaves).

Hint 22: Above the bakery, on the mural with green foliage, a tiny green classic Mickey is hiding just above the bottom rim, facing the wine cabinet.

Hint 23: Also in the food area, a classic Mickey hides in a leaf in the middle of the upper right mural of falling leaves.

Hint 24: As you enter the elevator to the Fitness Center, you can spot a classic Mickey on the lower left panel (as you face the rear of the elevator).

Hint 25: Many small classic Mickeys can be found in the carpet in the hallways in front of guest rooms. Classic Mickey images in the carpets below the 5th floor differ from those on and above the 5th floor.

- Kidani Village

Hint 26: A classic Mickey is at the 6:30 position on a large gold clock on a table just inside the entrance.

Hint 27: A white classic Mickey is on a ladybug on the middle level of the closest chandelier to the front lobby entrance.

Hint 28: At the entrance to Sanaa restaurant downstairs, a classic Mickey made of baskets is on the wall behind the check-in desk.

Hint 29: Inside Sanaa restaurant, a classic Mickey is above a booth on a white wall. It is to the left as you enter.

192

Hint 30: Classic Mickeys hide in the woodwork in the middle of Sanaa's dining tables.

Hint 31: Outside Sanaa, a classic Mickey is on the rockwork at the bottom rear of the lobby stairs.

(Other Hidden Mickeys are in the Spa and Health Club area, but only Kidani Village guests are allowed to enter there.)

Disney's All-Star Resorts

- All-Star Sports Resort

Hint 32: In the main building gift shop, classic Mickeys are part of the carpet. Each is composed of a baseball with two circles for ears.

Hint 33: Several classic Mickeys are on baseballs and basketballs on wall banners in the gift shop near the main lobby.

Hint 34: In the food court, a black classic Mickey is on the clock on the right wall along the queue for the basketball food order section.

Hint 35: Outside, behind and to the right of the registration building and past the buildings with surfboards, a large Mickey statue stands directly over a classic Mickey (white head and black ears) in the cement.

- All-Star Music Resort

Hint 36: In the Jazz Inn courtyard, classic Mickey ears top the cymbal stands. Each is a winged nut that holds a cymbal in place. (These nuts come and go.)

Hint 37: In the Country Fair area, you'll find classic Mickeys on the front and back of the huge boots.

- All-Star Movies Resort

Hint 38: The large checkers in Andy's Room in the "Toy Story" section sport classic Mickeys.

Coronado Springs Resort

Hint 39: A medallion on the left large, open wooden door at the front entrance to the main lobby is a three-dimensional relief of Mickey's face.

Hint 40: Another three-dimensional Mickey face is on the large right wooden door (as you face the doors) at the exit labeled El Centro.

Hint 41: In the hallway outside the Veracruz Exhibit Hall in the convention center, a black classic Mickey pattern repeats along the sides of some of the ceiling chandeliers. Nearby, a similar Mickey pattern can be spotted on rectangular light covers that are flush with the ceiling.

Hint 42: A classic Mickey is chipped into the cement by the lamppost nearest the Marina rental gazebo.

Hint 43: At the Dig Site swimming pool's main entrance (closest to the lake), a classic Mickey hides on a wall to your left before you enter. Check out the upper left part of the wall facing the lake.

Hint 44: After you enter the Dig Site, check out the upper left side of the wall to your left that faces the pool for another classic Mickey.

Hint 45: Also at the Dig Site, you'll find a whitish, somewhat distorted classic Mickey near the very top of the Mayan pyramid, on the side facing the pool. It's on the second stone block from the left, fourth row from the top.

Hint 46: Mickey Mouse (side profile) is sitting in a bus on some of the bus stop signs located around the periphery of the resort (such as at Bus Stop #4 between the Cabanas and Ranchos sections).

Pop Century Resort

Hint 47: In a small TV room near the check-in area, classic Mickey bubbles are under a fish in a fish bowl painted on the wall.

Hint 48: A tiny black classic Mickey is inside one or more round lights suspended from the ceiling in the Food Court area.

Hint 49: Several classic Mickeys are hiding on the tile floor of the food court order area. One is near the merchandise stand in the center of the order and pay area. Another is in front of the middle cash register.

Hint 50: A purple classic Mickey is on a purple wall near the "Classic Concoctions" sign, and a green classic Mickey is near the end of a green wall to the right of the food stations.

Hint 51: In the shop near the food court, classic Mickey holes are in the poles that hold merchandise racks.

Hint 52: Behind Roger Rabbit, in a mural on one of the '80s buildings near the Computer Pool, a classic Mickey is at the top of a bush beside a building. The bush's topmost leaf is just above Mickey's head and ears.

Hint 53: Look sharp for a lightly traced classic Mickey in green paint on an outside wall of the '60s building, behind the Mowgli figure and just past the Hippy Dippy Pool. It's on the left side of the wall with green plants, about halfway up the wall above a leaf and to the right of a brown tree.

Hint 54: In the guest laundry room near the Hippy Dippy Pool, a bubble classic Mickey is on the lower left of the painting of bubbles on the soap vending machine.

Hint 55: In the laundry room near the Bowling Pool, on the front of the soap vending machine and near the Soap Stop Vending Center sign, bubbles form two classic Mickeys at the lower right and one at the upper right.

Hint 56: Outside the main lobby, classic Mickeys are at the ends of the guardrails near the bus stops.

Caribbean Beach Resort

Hint 57: Behind Old Port Royale, a classic Mickey appears in the "Barefoot Bay Boat Yard" sign on the side of the lighthouse near the bike racks.

Hint 58: In the child's water play area near the main pool, a classic Mickey is on the helm near the wheel of the pirate ship.

Hint 59: At the main swimming pool, a tan classic Mickey is on the rockwork of the small slide's wall. To spot it, stand at the back of the pool and look under the left cannon.

Hint 60: In Shutters restaurant, a cloud classic Mickey is in a painting on the left wall of the room close to the rear exit door.

Downtown Disney Area Resorts

- Old Key West Resort

Hint 61: The design in the fence woodwork throughout Conch Flats General Store includes classic Mickeys.

Hint 62: Classic Mickeys are worked into the design of the fence railings behind the check-in counter in the registration area.

Hint 63: At the main pool (behind the registration building), the water slide (hidden in the rock) opens into the pool through the head of a classic Mickey.

Hint 64: At the upper right of the entrance to the steps to the water slide, a classic Mickey is indented in the white rock, above a space in the wall.

Hint 65: You'll see classic Mickeys in the railings outside, around the floors of the guest buildings.

Hints 66 and 67: Classic Mickeys formed by three shell imprints in the cement can be found on the two paths leading from parking spaces to Building 36. On the first path, you'll find the Hidden Mickey just after the first right turn on the right side. On the second path, the three shell imprints are in the corner of the sidewalk, after the first right turn and just before the next left turn.

- Port Orleans Resort – French Quarter

Hint 68: On the third painting from the left behind the registration counter, an upside-down classic Mickey is on a man's crown.

Hint 69: Upside-down classic Mickeys made of blue and white gemstones adorn the top of a crown hanging from the ceiling on the right side of the food court seating area.

- Port Orleans Resort – Riverside

Hint 70: Above the registration area, classic Mickeys are repeated in the wooden latticework circling the central lobby.

Hint 71: In the registration area, classic Mickeys decorate the sides of the brackets holding the giant fans hanging from the ceiling above the center of the lobby.

Hint 72: Classic Mickeys are at the base of the strapping on the big ceiling fans.

Hint 73: Classic Mickeys are in the soap bubbles on the Soap Stop Vending Center machine inside the Guest Laundry building by the pool to the right of Oak Manor.

Hint 74: Small classic Mickeys are in the upper level side rails at Parterre Place.

- Saratoga Springs Resort

Hint 75: Halfway down the hallway behind the Artist's Palette Shop (turn right as you enter the shop from the main lobby), a full-body impression of Mickey Mouse swinging a golf club is on a handle on the left door.

Hint 76: In the hallway leading to The Turf

Club, the jacket in a display on the left wall sports black classic Mickeys.

Hint 77: On a wall inside The Turf Club, Mickey and other Disney characters decorate billiard balls in the first display to the left as you enter from the hallway.

Hint 78: On a statue of a horse and rider outside the main lobby, the gear on both sides of the horse's mouth sports classic Mickeys. Tiny classic Mickeys are also hidden in the roses on both sides of the horse's winner's blanket. They are in the middle of the blanket in about the 3rd or 4th row down on either side of the horse. Finally, large blue classic Mickeys decorate the back and front of the jockey's jersey. (In addition, a blanket on the horse includes a yellow décor Mickey.)

Hint 79: As you walk away from the Artist's Palette, look for depressions in the left rock wall at the top of the stairs to the High Rock Spring Pool. One classic Mickey is in the middle of the top horizontal rock of the wall, and a second classic Mickey is on the lower horizontal rock near the handrail post.

Hint 80: The spa signs on the wall outside and on the glass door at the downstairs spa entrance have small classic Mickeys.

Hint 81: Some balcony railings on the guest buildings have classic Mickey holes.

Hint 82: In the resort's Springs section (Villas 4101-4436), across from the check-in parking lot, a large faint classic Mickey is on an outdoor red wall.

Hint 83: Classic Mickeys can be found in the upper corners of some of the outside lights on the guest buildings, such as on the exterior of the enclosed stairways.

Hint 84: Classic Mickeys are at the bottom of obelisks in the Villa courtyards.

Hint 85: Partial classic Mickeys are in the left side of the gate to the Grandstand pool and on the back gate next to the restrooms.

Epcot Resorts

- BoardWalk Resort

Hint 86: In the main lobby, an outside horse on the small carousel has brown spots that form two classic Mickeys, one on the neck and one on the thigh.

Hint 87: In the middle painting on the wall above the middle registration counter in the main lobby, a classic Mickey is formed by the second small group of trees from the right.

Hint 88: Classic Mickeys hold the shades in place on the lamps facing the fireplace in the center of the lobby.

Hint 89: Classic Mickeys hide in the carpet in front of some elevators and also appear in the guest room hallway carpets in both the BoardWalk Inn and BoardWalk Villas. Tinker Bell is on a carpet in front of an elevator in the BoardWalk Inn.

Hint 90: The carpet outside the elevators on the lobby floor of the BoardWalk Villas sports many images: A blue classic Mickey, Minnie's shoes, Pluto's footprints, Goofy's hat and shoes, and Donald's cap and footprints.

Hint 91: On the sign over the entrance to Seashore Sweets, a cloud classic Mickey is in the sky between the two ladies, next to the head of the lady on the left.

- Beach Club Resort

Hint 92: Along the inside walkway in front of the Cape May Café, a full length Mickey Mouse is standing in a sandcastle. It's the sculpture farthest to the left, on the wall facing the pool.

Hint 93: Enter the Solarium from the Beach Club main lobby. The first painting on the wall to your left has Mickey's face on spare tires on the backs of the yellow car (left side) and the blue car (right side).

Hint 94: Classic Mickey hood ornaments adorn the blue and red cars on the right of this painting.

Hint 95: In the second painting on the left wall, you can see Mickey's face looking out at you from the clouds at the upper right.

Hint 96: In this second painting, a lady on the beach is sitting on a Mickey Mouse towel.

Hint 97: The cruise ship smokestacks in this second painting have classic Mickey decals.

Hint 98: Mickey balloons are on the right side of the third painting to your left.

Hint 99: Also on the right side of this third painting is a tiny white classic Mickey atop the front post of a small building with a brown roof.

Hint 100: The guest room hallways have carpet segments with classic Mickeys, some inside seashells.

Hint 101: Classic Mickeys are in the wallpaper along the guest room hallways.

Hint 102: Some of the bubbles (only a few!) in the carpets near the lobby elevators form classic Mickeys. A strange purple classic Mickey (disguised as a sea urchin?) also floats around in the rug.

Hint 103: Sand dollars form classic Mickeys in the carpet of the Marketplace shop.

Hint 104: Under the Ariel Statue in front of the entrance to the Beach Club Villas, seashells are embedded in the ground. One group of three shells forms a classic Mickey.

Hint 105: At Cape May Café, a display on the wall behind the check-in podium usually has a Hidden Mickey or other hidden characters made of crayons. This image changes from time to time.

Hint 106: In the Beaches & Cream Soda Shop, onion rings form a classic Mickey.

He's on the left wall as you enter, on the second panel back from the rear wall.

- Yacht Club Resort

Hint 107: On the globe in the main lobby, a blue classic Mickey is at the bottom right-hand corner of the sea monster, under the sea monster's head and below the island of Madagascar.

Hint 108: In a seating area in the main lobby, the names of Mickey, Minnie, Donald, Daisy, Goofy, and Huey are on small labels on the drawers of a corner cabinet. (This cabinet is moved around at times to different parts of the lobby.)

Hint 109: Near the main lobby seating area, dark classic Mickeys are in the rug.

Hint 110: The rug near the elevator on various floors has classic Mickeys in the corners.

Hint 111: Various other classic Mickey images can be found in other carpets around the resort, especially near elevators and in the guest hallways.

Hint 112: A photo of (now deceased) Minnie Moo, a cow born with a black classic Mickey on her side, often hangs in the Yachtsman Steakhouse. Examine the left wall just past the entrance podium. Minnie Moo once resided at Fort Wilderness.

Fort Wilderness Resort

Hint 113: Another photograph of Minnie Moo (see above) is on the wall in a display room to the right at the entrance to the Tri-Circle D Ranch Horse Barn.

Hint 114: A classic Mickey brand is on the left side of the Blacksmith sign near the Horse Barn.

Hint 115: At the front parking lot, two Hidden Mickeys are on the Fort Wilderness Kennel sign. They are in the scrollwork underneath the word "Club," one on the left and one on the right.

Wilderness Lodge Resort

Hint 116: On the right side of the entrance drive to the hotel, a full length Mickey Mouse is walking on top of the "Bear Crossing" sign.

Hint 117: A classic Mickey is on the slanted end of the first horizontal log beam of the guard gate kiosk as your car approaches the entrance gate.

Hint 118: As you approach the center steps from the parking lot, you'll see that the roof of the covered unloading area in front of the entrance is supported by huge wooden logs, banded together (four to a set) by black metal strips. The right rear pole of the first set to the right (as you face the entrance) has a classic Mickey etched in the wood above the upper black metal band. This Mickey faces the parking lot.

Hint 119: In the set of support poles on the left after you walk up the center steps from the parking lot, the pole in the corner closest to you and the entrance to the hotel has a classic Mickey etched in the wood. This Mickey is partially covered by the upper black metal band; only his head and part of his right ear are visible. This Mickey faces the steps.

Hint 120: In the cement of the car entrance drive-through, the black stripe nearest the center steps from the parking lot has a tiny classic Mickey. From the red rectangle in the cement, follow the right (as you face the hotel entrance) diagonal crack to the black stripe. The tiny classic Mickey is traced in the cement about six inches to the right of the intersection of the crack and the stripe.

Hint 121: As you face the hotel entrance, the left rear support pole of the far left set of poles closest to the parking lot has a classic Mickey etched in the wood. It's above the lateral crossbeam on the lower part of the pole.

Hint 122: A classic Mickey hides on the left side of a large key in a wall display behind the registration counter. Look near the entrance to the Mercantile Shop.

202

Hint 123: A sign that says "Walt Disney World Transportation" hangs from the ceiling near the Mercantile Shop. Mickey (in side profile) is driving the bus at the top of the sign.

Hint 124: In the lobby, you'll find a classic Mickey on the rock in the corner to the upper right of the fireplace. Search at the level of and near the lower round wooden horizontal beam that juts toward the lobby.

Hint 125: The outer grillwork of a fireplace in the rear room of the Whispering Canyon Café is adorned with decorative cutouts. Bend down low and look for a classic Mickey on the bottom row. It is the third cutout from the left corner.

Hint 126: At the entrance stairs to the Territory Lounge, a classic Mickey decorates a pot in the right lower section of a wall map.

Hint 127: Inside the Territory Lounge, you'll find a classic Mickey on the rear of a beige mule in a ceiling mural. Look above the center of the bar.

Hint 128: Inside the Artist Point restaurant, examine the large mural above the entrance to the rear left dining area. You can spot a classic Mickey in the upper part of the lowest tree on the right if you look between the third and fourth lights (counting from the left) illuminating the mural.

Hint 129: Also in the rear left dining area, the top middle part of a dark cloud in a painting on the left wall is shaped like a side profile of Winnie the Pooh (he's looking to the right).

Hint 130: A display case on an inside wall facing the entrance to the Roaring Fork snack bar contains three chestnuts arranged to form a classic Mickey.

Hint 131: A few wall-light covers have classic Mickey images (especially the sideways Mickey image at the lower center of the light cover). Some of these covers are near the elevators just past Roaring Fork snack area, and one or more can be found elsewhere around the hotel.

Hint 132: The wallpaper in the guest hallways on most floors (for example, near the elevators) includes classic Mickeys in the design.

Hint 133: Segments of the guest hallway carpets contain blue classic Mickeys.

Hint 134: A classic Mickey is etched near the bottom of a flat vertical wooden post around the corner from Room 6100 and near a green EXIT sign.

Hint 135: Near room 5066, a classic Mickey is etched on a flat, wooden vertical post about five and a half feet from the floor. It's across from an ice machine.

Hint 136: A classic Mickey is etched on a vertical wooden post about six feet up from the floor across from Room 4035.

Hint 137: Outside, from the walkway next to Fire Rock Geyser, scan the shallow stream running down from the small pool by the geyser. You'll find a slightly distorted classic Mickey with white rocks for ears in the rock of the streambed about a third of the way up to the geyser.

Hint 138: Walk toward the Boat and Bike Rental and locate stairs to an exit door in the corner of the main building. A classic Mickey is imprinted in a vertical wooden beam at the left side of the exit door (as you face the door) across from the fourth-floor balcony. Mickey is on the right side of the beam, just below the log that juts out to the right.

- in the Cub's Den

Hint 139: A plush Mickey doll sits in the rightmost teepee in the mural on the right wall.

Hint 140: In this same mural, a side-profile shadow of Mickey (standing and looking right) falls on the side of a mountain to the right of the center of the mural and above the tree line.

Hint 141: On the far left of this mural, about midway up and left of the mountains, you can spot a classic Mickey.

- Wilderness Lodge Villas

Hint 142: Inside and to the left of the entrance to the Wilderness Lodge Villas, a classic Mickey decorates the wall near the lower left corner of a picture frame to the right of the elevators. Two more classic Mickeys are part of the wall decoration between the elevators.

Hint 143: Mickey Mouse is peeking out of a hole on the outer side of the first overhead beam to your right as you enter the lobby of the Wilderness Lodge Villas. The beam is jutting out into the lobby and has a rattlesnake on top.

Hint 144: A side profile of Mickey Mouse is on the upper part of a wall, between two moons, near the lobby of the Wilderness Lodge Villas and to the right as you enter the lobby.

Magic Kingdom Monorail Resorts

- Polynesian Resort

Hint 145: On the lower level, just inside the main lobby, there's a classic Mickey design in the flagstone tiles a few feet in front of the waterfall.

Hint 146: Near the various entrances and inside the Tiki Boutique store on the first floor, three wooden statues holding merchandise have classic Mickeys; two are blue and white while the third is red.

Hint 147: A slightly distorted green classic Mickey image is on the upper back of the Tiki statue outside the Tiki Boutique shop on the first floor. Many folks stop here for photos with the smiling Tiki guy.

Hint 148: Several different classic Mickeys are in the carpet on the first floor near the Wyland Gallery and to the right of the gallery entrance.

Hint 149: Along the corner staircase from the lobby, wall decorations have bamboo rings. Seen end on, some of the lower rings in the rightside decoration form classic Mickeys.

Hint 150: In Trader Jack's gift shop, Mickey Mouse is sitting in a chair on top of some merchandise cabinets. He's in front of the upper wall mural.

Hint 151: You'll find classic Mickeys on the arms of that chair.

Hint 152: In the carpet on the second floor near and to the right of Trader Jack's shop, a brown classic Mickey is in the border and a blue classic Mickey is on a turtle shell. A similar carpet with these two Hidden Mickeys is in the kids' craft area on the first floor near the front entrance.

Hint 153: At the Kona Island coffee bar, in front of the Kona Café, small purple tiles on top of the mosaic tile counter form a classic Mickey. You'll spot it to the left of the glass case.

Hint 154: On the "Order Here" screen at Captain Cook's snack bar, images pan from right to left. As the image moves right, look for a palm tree with Mickey's shadow on its trunk.

Hint 155: Near Captain Cook's snack bar, the sign above the entrance for Moana Mickey's Arcade bears a classic Mickey on the top end of Mickey's spear.

Hint 156: The carpet in some of the hallways and elevators sports classic Mickeys.

- Wedding Pavilion

Hint 157: The weather vane on top of the building closest to the monorail has a full-length side profile of Mickey Mouse.

- Grand Floridian Resort

206 Hint 158: Weather vanes on various roofs at the front of the resort sport classic Mickeys.

Hint 159: The large trolley carts outside the hotel have classic Mickeys in the woodwork around the luggage storage areas at the back of the carts.

Hint 160: Along the entrance hall to 1900 Park Fare restaurant, a Mickey hat image is at the left lower corner of the left lower picture in a group of carousel pictures on the wall.

Hint 161: In the main lobby, gold classic Mickeys are in the carpet.

Hint 162: The staircase on the right side of the lobby as you enter from the front has carpeting with classic Mickeys along its outer borders.

Hint 163: In the ironwork of the elevator enclosure between the floors, four classic Mickey images are at the intersection of the diagonal spokes and the large circle. Stand inside the main lobby elevator for the best view of this classic Mickey.

Hint 164: Most guest room hallways have classic Hidden Mickeys in the wallpaper.

Hint 165: Classic Mickeys are also in the guest hallway carpets.

Hint 166: Inside Gasparilla Grill & Games, two classic Mickey images are in the third picture on the wall to the left above the restrooms. One is formed by a coin and two rings and another is on a silver utensil.

Hint 167: In the lobbies of the outer guest buildings, the carpets have Hidden Mickeys as well as a Hidden Minnie Mouse, Donald Duck, Goofy, and Pluto.

- Contemporary Resort

Hint 168: From the window of the California Grill restaurant on the hotel's top floor, you can see a stretched out Mickey watchband on the ground in front of the building. It's among the conical-shaped trees. (You can see part of this watchband from the monorail.)

Hint 169: Inside the California Grill, the top of a classic Mickey is frosted in the design of the (closed) glass doors of the back room.

Hint 170: From the sixth floor outdoor balcony closest to the front of the hotel, look left to see Mickey sitting on the edge of a roof below! This Mickey can also be spotted from either monorail just outside the hotel (the opening nearest the Transportation and Ticket Center). If you're on the resort monorail, you have to bend down to view Mickey through the lower part of the window (to the left of forward motion) and below the express monorail track next to you. On the express monorail, look to the right of forward motion.

Hint 171: Inside Chef Mickey's restaurant, a large side-profile Mickey decorates both sides of the large black, white, and red tile divider.

Hint 172: Ice cube trays on a shelf against the large central yellow pillar of Chef Mickey's buffet area have classic Mickey indentations.

Hint 173: Mickey ears are atop posts at the rear of Chef Mickey's restaurant.

Hint 174: On the lower part of the wall mural facing Contempo Café, the fourth girl from the right corner of the wall has a classic Mickey on her dress.

Hint 175: High on the wall mural facing Bay Lake, a black classic Mickey is on an owl perched on a girl's head. It's on the red right wing (as you face the mural).

Hint 176: On the fourth floor, a stick figure Mickey is in an artwork display on the side of the BVG Store facing the monorail.

Hint 177: On the fourth floor, classic Mickeys are in the carpet inside The Game Station arcade.

Hint 178: Behind the main hotel, a classic Mickey silhouette can be found in the bricks under the metal Mickey Mouse sculpture. (The sculpture itself is a decorative Mickey, not a Hidden Mickey.)

Hint 179: In The Sand Bar by the pool, near the middle of the upper left wall border, one of the semaphore figures is wearing Mickey ears.

Hint 180: At the exit from the Garden Building to the parking lot (facing the monorail), a huge classic Mickey is traced in the tile under the exit canopy between the benches.

Shades of Green Resort

Hint 181: In the Shades of Green lobby, a Mickey statue stands in front of a framed picture of a blue sky with puffy clouds. Three classic Mickeys are in the clouds and another, made of fireworks, decorates the statue Mickey's right ear.

Hint 182: The Millpond pool is shaped as a classic Mickey. You can visit this pool outside or spot it on a resort map posted on hallway walls.

Notes

CHAPTER 7

Hither, Thither & Yon Scavenger Hunt

A car is the most efficient method for hunting the following areas. I've planned the hunt taking time of day and location into consideration. However, some backtracking will help keep you ahead of the crowds. Don't forget to be courteous to the shoppers, diners, golfers, swimmers, other guests, and Cast Members you encounter during your hunt. (Because you may want to hunt only one area at a time, I've listed the perfect score for each area in parentheses after its name in the Clues section.)

WDW Golf Courses
(10 points)

If you're a golfer, look for the following Hidden Mickeys:

Clue 1: A classic Mickey sand trap on the Magnolia Golf Course.
5 points

Clue 2: A putting green shaped like Mickey Mouse at the Osprey Ridge Golf Club. You can visit this Hidden Mickey without playing golf.
5 points

Walt Disney World Speedway
(5 points)

Clue 3: Go to the racetrack to take a look at the lake on the infield, or more accurately, a photo of it. The lake is barely visible from the fence around the parking area for the *Richard Petty Driving Experience*. So check out a framed photo of the racetrack inside the guest sign-in building to find this classic Mickey.
5 points

211

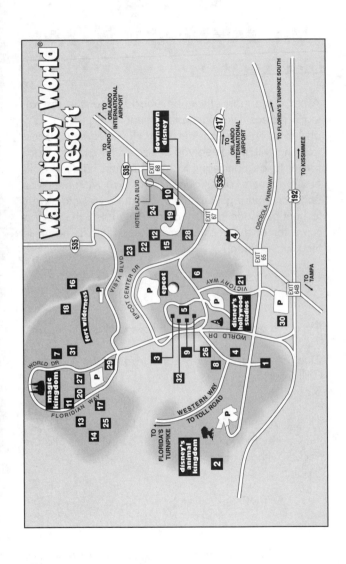

1 All-Star Resorts
2 Animal Kingdom Lodge
3 Beach Club
4 Blizzard Beach
5 BoardWalk
6 Caribbean Beach
7 Contemporary
8 Coronado Springs
9 Dolphin
10 Downtown Disney
11 Grand Floridian
12 Lake Buena Vista Golf Course
13 Magnolia Golf Course
14 Oak Trails Golf Course
15 Old Key West
16 Osprey Ridge Golf Course
17 Palm Golf Course

18 Pioneer Hall
19 Pleasure Island, in Downtown Disney
20 Polynesian
21 Pop Century
22 Port Orleans – French Quarter
23 Port Orleans – Riverside
24 Saratoga Springs
25 Shades of Green
26 Swan
27 Transportation and Ticket Center
28 Typhoon Lagoon
29 WDW Speedway
30 Wide World of Sports
31 Wilderness Lodge
32 Yacht Club
P Parking

WDW Water Parks
(41 points)

★ *Blizzard Beach* (21 points)

Clue 4: Take a close look at the Beach Haus store's right rear wall near the dressing rooms.
3 points

Clue 5: In the Lottawatta Lodge counter-service restaurant, find a classic Mickey above the fireplace.
4 points

Clue 6: Look for a "Hidden Lizard" in the rocks behind *Melt-Away Bay.*
4 points

Clue 7: Hop on the *Chairlift* to spot a classic Mickey formed by three round rocks on the ground near one of the support poles for the ride. (Tip: The Singles line for the *Chairlift* is usually shorter than the regular line.)
5 points

Clue 8: Go to the rear of the park (by tube or on foot) to find a classic Mickey with a sorcerer's hat that's formed by three stones topped by a small triangular rock. Psst! He's near the center of the side of a stone bridge that crosses over *Cross Country Creek.*
5 points

★ *Typhoon Lagoon* (20 points)

Clue 9: Look around the *Crush 'n' Gusher* elevator for a Hidden Mickey.
4 points

Clue 10: Search for Mickey on a bridge over *Castaway Creek,* near *Shark Reef.*
4 points

Clue 11: Don't pass by Mickey on the steps up to the *Storm Slides.*
4 points

 Clue 12: Spot the Main Mouse hiding under

a cannon along *Castaway Creek* at the rear of the park.
4 points

Clue 13: Squint for Mickey in the wall of a cave at *Ketchakiddee Creek*.
4 points

Disney's Wide World of Sports
(10 points)

Clue 14: Search hard for a three-dimensional Mickey Mouse head near the high central ceiling of The Milk House (the Field House). He's on an upper rafter opposite the main entrance. Hard to find but worth it!
5 points

Clue 15: Don't miss Mickey in the outfield!
5 points

Downtown Disney West Side
(52 points)

★ *Cirque du Soleil* (8 points)

Clue 16: Look down for a Hidden Mickey in the sidewalk near Parking Lot Q.
5 points

Clue 17: Head for the outside restrooms (they're under the main entrance staircase to the theater) and examine the floor in either one (men's or women's). See a small classic Mickey?
3 points for either

★ *House of Blues* (3 points)

Clue 18: Search for a classic Mickey on the ceiling.
3 points

★ *DisneyQuest* (29 points)

Clue 19: Toward the end of the pre-show video, during the entrance elevator ride, find a classic Mickey formed by three small spheres.
3 points

215

Clue 20: Check out the carpets on the third and fifth floors (in, respectively, Ventureport and The Food-Quest dining area).
3 points for spotting both

Clue 21: Look for track lighting shaped like a classic Mickey on the second through fifth floors. Psst! It's not on the same side on all four floors.
5 points for spotting all four

Clue 22: Find similar lighting near "Invasion! An Extra-TERRORestrial Alien Encounter."
3 points

Clue 23: Spot classic Mickey markings on the back of one of the creatures you encounter during "Aladdin's Magic Carpet Ride." (You don't have to take the ride; you can watch the overhead video screens as others ride.)
4 points

★ Find two classic Hidden Mickeys at the "Virtual Jungle Cruise." (Again, you needn't take the ride; you can stand behind one of the ride pods and watch.)

Clue 24: Before the ride starts, watch the left side of the screen.
4 points

Clue 25: Keep watching the screen during the first part of the ride to see if the raft exits a glacier area. (The riders have optional routes, so they may not enter the glacier area.) If it does, watch carefully as it exits. (The ears on this Hidden Mickey aren't perfectly formed, but you'll recognize them.)
3 points

Clue 26: Along the queue for "Pirates of the Caribbean," examine the walls for Hidden Mickeys.
2 points

Clue 27: Check out the trash can and the floor at the exit.
2 points for spotting both

★ *Wolfgang Puck Café* (5 points)

Clue 28: Study the mosaic tile pyramid behind

the reception counter to find a classic Hidden Mickey.
5 points

★ *Disney's Candy Cauldron* (4 points)

Clue 29: Go inside to find a classic Mickey marking on a stone.
4 points

★ *Mickey's Groove* (1 point)

Clue 30: Observe the logo.
1 point

★ *Pleasure Island Bus Stop* (2 points)

Clue 31: Look down near one of the bus stops.
2 points

Downtown Disney Marketplace
(150 points)

★ *Entrance to the Marketplace* (3 points)

Clue 32: Check out the signs over the entrances.
1 point for one or more

Clue 33: Study the green benches for Hidden Mickeys at the entrance and elsewhere around the Marketplace.
2 points

★ *Disney's Wonderful World of Memories store* (3 points)

Clue 34: Search for Mickey outside the store.
3 points

★ *Disney's Days of Christmas* (6 points)

Clue 35: Step inside and find at least one classic Mickey on each of three large trees.
4 points total for one or more on each tree

Clue 36: Take a good look at the ceiling in the rear room of the shop.
2 points

217

★ *Goofy's Candy Co.* (10 points)

Clue 37: Search for a Goofy shadow in the store.
4 points

Clue 38: Look for Goofy and other characters on the wall.
4 points for three or more characters

Clue 39: Find Mickey in a store window.
2 points

★ *Mickey's Mart* — a.k.a. *"Everything Ten Dollars and under"* (2 points)

Clue 40: Glance up for some Hidden Mickeys above an entrance.
2 points

★ *Marketplace Carrousel* (5 points)

Clue 41: Study the decorative panels on the Carrousel for four classic Mickeys.
5 points for four classic Mickeys

★ *Mickey's Pantry* (3 points)

Clue 42: Spot classic Mickeys on the walls.
3 points for three or more

★ *Once Upon A Toy* (35 points)

(This store sports numerous Mickeys and other Disney characters in the décor in addition to Hidden Mickeys.)

Clue 43: Examine the interactive fountain near the store. (Note: Two Hidden Mickeys are there all the time, a third appears only when the water is on.)
4 points for two, 5 points for spotting all three

Clue 44: Find classic Mickeys in the cement outside.
2 points

Clue 45: Examine the snowflakes in a window display.
Psst! Look for two types of Hidden Mickeys.
3 points for spotting both

Clue 46: Outside the main entrance, look for classic Mickeys with tires for ears.
2 points

★ Now enter the store and keep your eyes open.

Clue 47: Gaze up for two Hidden Mickeys (one full-body Mickey is on a classic Mickey).
5 points for spotting both

Clue 48: Check out the tops of merchandise stands. Psst! Only some sport Hidden Mickeys.
1 point

Clue 49: Now examine the bottoms of these stands.
1 point

Clue 50: Look at the upper beams of the wooden merchandise displays.
1 point

Clue 51: Now observe the bolts on those displays.
1 point

Clue 52: Search for a classic Mickey on a sandal in the middle of the first room.
3 points

Clue 53: Examine the mural behind the service desk in the same room.
1 point

Clue 54: Find a classic Hidden Mickey cloud in a central room.
3 points

Clue 55: Look for a Mickey shadow in a central room.
3 points

Clue 56: Say hello to a big bear wearing Hidden Mickeys.
2 points

Clue 57: Look for Hidden Mickey lollipops.
2 points

★ *Disney's Pin Traders* (3 points)

Clue 58: Spot a Mickey on a statue inside the store.
3 points

★ *Team Mickey Athletic Club* (8 points)

Clue 59: Find a Hidden Mickey in the Disney Vacation Club (DVC) display near Team Mickey.
2 points

Clue 60: Observe the pillars outside.
1 point

Clue 61: Inside the store, check the tops of the mannequin heads and merchandise stands.
2 points for two types

Clue 62: Search for a classic Mickey near some golf clubs.
3 points

★ *Ghirardelli Ice Cream and Chocolate Shop* (8 points)

Clue 63: Stare at the outside ironwork for a classic Mickey.
4 points

Clue 64: Locate Mickey on a wall inside.
4 points

★ *Near the lake* (3 points)

Clue 65: Do you see any chairs outside the Ghirardelli Shop with Hidden Mickeys?
2 points

Clue 66: Spot Mickeys in the fence around the lake.
1 point

★ *World of Disney* (51 points)

Clue 67: Look up for Mickeys on the store sign.
1 point

Clue 68: Find light brown Mickeys outside the store.
2 points

Clue 69: Check out a display window for characters on a map.
4 points for four characters

Clue 70: Search for Mickey ears in another display window.
4 points

Clue 71: Look for classic Mickeys in some of the clothing racks.
2 points

Clue 72: Examine some of the indoor signs for an image of Mickey.
2 points

Clue 73: Look closely at a map on a cashier's counter.
4 points for three or more

Clue 74: Find a classic Mickey emblem on the Chinese Theater in a wall mural in the high-ceilinged central room.
4 points

Clue 75: In the same room, find an upside-down classic Mickey on the Pocahontas airship.
4 points

★ Now find two classic Mickeys on the Tweedle Dee and Tweedle Dum mural in the same room.

Clue 76: Look for a flag.
2 points

Clue 77: Check out an apron.
2 points

Clue 78: Now study the mannequins.
4 points

Clue 79: Spot classic Mickeys on paintings in the central Genie Room.
2 points

221

Clue 80: Now look carefully for Hidden Mickeys in the central Genie room's wallpaper.
3 points

Clue 81: In the same room, observe the "antique" maps decorating the walls. Psst! Think character profiles.
5 points for three or more

Clue 82: Next door in the Villain Room, spot Cruella DeVille's Hidden Mickey.
3 points

Clue 83: Outside the store, in an entrance area to the Marketplace, look around for a classic Mickey.
3 points

★ *LEGO Imagination Center* (5 points)

Clue 84: Outside the store, search for a classic Mickey on a LEGO object.
5 points

★ *T-Rex Café* (5 points)

Clue 85: Admire a classic Mickey near the bar area.
5 points

WDW Casting Center
(3 points)

Clue 86: Drive to the Casting building, across the road from the rightmost Downtown Disney Marketplace entrance, to locate classic Mickeys. (These Hidden Mickeys can also be spotted from Interstate 4).
3 points

Miniature Golf Courses
(15 points)

You can find Hidden Mickeys while you play the courses. Or you may be able to walk the courses without playing if it's not crowded, due to rain or luck. (Tell the attendants that you're hunting Hidden Mickeys and ask if you can take a look around.)

★ *Fantasia Gardens* (4 points)

Clue 87: Check the tee-off areas.
1 point

Clue 88: Take a good look at the 12th hole on the Gardens Course.
3 points

★ **Winter Summerland** (11 points)

Clue 89: Find Mickey on the third hole.
3 points

★ Now head straight for the 16th holes.

Clue 90: Spot Goofy and Donald on the 16th hole of the Winter Course.
3 points

Clue 91: Now check around the same hole for a Mickey Mouse gingerbread cookie.
2 points

Clue 92: Find Mickey and Minnie on the 16th hole of the Summer Course. Psst! This Hidden Mickey is also visible from the 16th and 17th holes of the Winter Course.
3 points

Near Celebration, Florida
(4 points)

Okay, I admit it; this Mickey isn't hidden. Just the opposite, in fact. But it is unique. So I decided to include it anyway. You'll find a huge classic Mickey near Celebration, Florida, on the west side of Interstate 4.

Clue 93: Look for it as you get close to Exit 62.
4 points

Near the Magic Kingdom
(5 points)

Clue 94: You can only see this classic Mickey made of tree groves from the air or on an image from a Google search. It's a few miles northwest of the Magic Kingdom. Good luck!
5 points

Total Points for Hither, Thither & Yon =

How'd you do?

A perfect score for this hunt is 295, but here is a break-down by area, so that you can tally your score for only those areas you've covered. Give yourself gold if you score at least 80% of available points.

The Golf Courses (10)
Walt Disney World Speedway (5)
The Water Parks (41)
   Blizzard Beach (21)
   Typhoon Lagoon (20)
Disney's Wide World of Sports (10)
Downtown Disney West Side (52)
   Cirque du Soleil (8)
   House of Blues (3)
   DisneyQuest (29)
   Wolfgang Puck Café (5)
   Disney's Candy Cauldron (4)
   Mickey's Groove (1)
   Pleasure Island Bus Stop (2)
Downtown Disney Marketplace (150)
   Entrance to the Marketplace (3)
   Disney's Wonderful World of Memories store (3)
   Disney's Days of Christmas (6)
   Goofy's Candy Co. (10)
   Mickey's Mart (2)
   Marketplace Carrousel (5)
   Mickey's Pantry (3)
   Once Upon A Toy (35)
   Disney's Pin Traders (3)
   Team Mickey Athletic Club (8)
   Ghirardelli Ice Cream and Chocolate Shop (8)
   Near the lake (3)
   World of Disney (51)
   LEGO Imagination Center (5)
   T-Rex Café (5)
WDW Casting Center (3)
Miniature Golf Courses (15)
   Fantasia Gardens (4)
   Winter Summerland (11)
   Near Celebration, Florida (4)
   Near the Magic Kingdom (5)

**Caution:
Don't peek at this
section unless you
really want help!**

The Golf Courses

Hint 1: A sand trap at the sixth green of the Magnolia Golf Course is shaped like a classic Mickey.

Hint 2: The practice putting green at Osprey Ridge Golf Club is shaped like a side profile of Mickey Mouse.

Walt Disney World Speedway

Hint 3: A lake on the infield is shaped like a classic Mickey. You'll barely see the lake, let alone the Hidden Mickey, from ground level. To marvel at its full effect without paying admission, walk inside the guest sign-in building and look at the framed photo on the wall.

Water Parks

- Blizzard Beach

Hint 4: Find a lighting fixture on the wall at

the right rear of the Beach Haus store near the dressing rooms. There's a painting on the cover in which a small classic Mickey is formed by rocks at the lower center of an outdoor mountain scene.

Hint 5: Above the fireplace near the food order area in the Lottawatta Lodge counter-service restaurant, a classic Mickey is formed by three stones in the center of the chimney, about halfway between the mantelpiece and the ceiling.

Hint 6: At the top of the rocky hill at the rear of *Melt-Away Bay*, just right of center, the highest rock forms a lizard's snout. His left front foot is visible on the rock below.

Hint 7: From the *Chairlift* ride that takes you to the water slides, look to the ground on the second level of the mountain just past support pole #4 (counting from the beginning of the lift) to spot a classic Mickey made of three round rocks.

Hint 8: At the rear of the park, a classic Mickey is formed by three stones jutting out from near the top edge of a stone bridge crossing *Cross Country Creek*. It is on the side of the bridge, near the center. A small triangular rock over this Hidden Mickey gives it the appearance of wearing a sorcerer's hat.

You can see this Mickey from the water or dry land. It's visible from the floating tubes as you approach the bridge and, on land, you can see it through the trees either from in front of the *Runoff Rapids* entrance sign or from several points on the walkway on the other side of the bridge.

- Typhoon Lagoon

Hint 9: At *Crush 'n' Gusher*, on the upper floor near the elevator, paint circles on the cement form a classic Mickey.

Hint 10: Mickey ears are at the bottom of a vertical strut in the railing of a bridge. You can see the ears if you enter *Castaway Creek* at Shark Landing (near *Shark Reef*) and look behind you as you float under the first bridge. The ears are toward the right side of the bridge. You can also see the ears if you walk across the bridge, then walk downstream on the path and look back.

Hint 11: About halfway up the wooden steps to the *Storm Slides*, Mickey ears are on the left side of a walkway slat, just before the large anchor on the right side of the path.

Hint 12: A classic Mickey formed by cannonballs is on your left under the first cannon past the waterfall if you're drifting in the creek. If you're walking on the nearby trail, this classic Mickey is just past Forgotten Grotto in the rear of the park as you walk alongside the drifters.

Hint 13: In the walk-through cave at the rear of *Ketchakiddee Creek*, a classic Mickey hole is in the rock. It's on the back wall of the cave, about one and a half feet up from the ground, and near the drain at the right side of the cave as you enter the cave from the water.

Disney's Wide World of Sports

Hint 14: A three-dimensional Mickey Mouse head looks out over the court from near the high central ceiling in The Milk House (the Field House). He's on an upper rafter above the sign, "The Milk House," in front of a yellow triangular wall partition that is opposite the main entrance. I spotted him to the upper left of the lower seats of section 104.

Hint 15: A large, pale green classic Mickey image lies in the outfield grass in the Wide World of Sports baseball stadium.

Downtown Disney West Side

- *Cirque du Soleil*

Hint 16: A classic Mickey is etched in the sidewalk near Cirque du Soleil, on the second slab back from Parking Lot Q, just past a manhole cover and near the grass.

Hint 17: Under the main entrance staircase to the *Cirque du Soleil* show are restrooms for men and women. You will find tiles laid to approximate a small classic Hidden Mickey on the floor of each restroom, in a corner just inside the entrance doors. These circles don't touch, but the design is convincing enough for my eyes.

- House of Blues

Hint 18: Walk through the front door and down the right side aisle. A classic Mickey is on the ceiling past the first server's station.

- DisneyQuest

Hint 19: Toward the end of the pre-show video, during the entrance elevator ride, a classic Mickey is formed by three spheres at the bottom of a ray gun. (This Hidden Mickey is more convincing than the spheres at the bottom of the large three-dimensional ray gun poised over the lobby of Ventureport.)

Hint 20: Symbols and figures that include classic Mickey designs are woven into the carpets on the third and fifth floors in, respectively, Ventureport and The FoodQuest dining area.

Hint 21: Track lighting shaped like a classic Mickey hangs above the elevator doors on floors two, three, four, and five. You'll find it near the "Mighty Ducks Pinball Slam" (on the third floor) and near "Ride the Comix" (on the fourth and fifth floors). On the second floor, near "CyberSpace Mountain," the lighting is above an elevator door on the opposite side of the elevator bank.

Hint 22: Similar track lighting can be found in front of pod 4 of "Invasion! An ExtraTERRORestrial Alien Encounter."

Hint 23: During "Aladdin's Magic Carpet Ride," the golden beetle you encounter bears classic Mickey markings on its back.

Hint 24: At the "Virtual Jungle Cruise," classic Mickey-shaped balloons periodically float up from the left side of the screen, in front of the castle, before the ride starts.

Hint 25: On the screen in the first part of the "Virtual Jungle Cruise" ride, the raft may exit a glacier area under a distorted classic Mickey-shaped ice bridge over the river.

Hint 26: In the wall murals along the queue for "Pirates of the Caribbean," the rightmost set of palm tree coconuts near the stairs is shaped like a classic Mickey.

Hint 27: The DisneyQuest classic Mickey logo is on trash cans (like the one near the exit) and is illuminated on the floor of the exit walkway.

- Wolfgang Puck Café

Hint 28: Behind the reception counter, about two thirds of the way up the mosaic pyramid, a white tile and two smaller black tiles form a classic Mickey. Search for it to the right of a tall ceramic vessel standing on a shelf.

- Disney's Candy Cauldron

Hint 29: Inside the store, on the upper wall above the candy display, a dark marking on a stone near the ceiling forms a classic Hidden Mickey.

- Mickey's Groove

Hint 30: Above the entrance doors, a classic Mickey forms the middle of the Mickey's Groove logo.

- Pleasure Island Bus Stop

Hint 31: A large classic Mickey is in the cement between Bus Stops 5 and 6, across from Planet Hollywood restaurant.

Downtown Disney Marketplace

- *Entrance to the Marketplace*

Hint 32: Signs over the entrances to the Marketplace sport classic Mickeys at their sides.

Hint 33: Green benches with classic Mickey emblems on the top and sides are scattered around the Marketplace and the interactive fountain.

- *Disney's Wonderful World of Memories*

Hint 34: The sign on the store contains a full-figure Hidden Mickey on the page of a book.

- *Disney's Days of Christmas*

Hint 35: Inside the shop, three large trees surrounded by merchandise have classic Mickeys carved in their bark near the tops of their trunks. The trees are not Christmas trees, and each of the three has one or two Mickey carvings.

Hint 36: In the rear room of the shop, classic Mickeys are in the scrollwork on the ceiling.

- *Goofy's Candy Co.*

Hint 37: A shadow of Goofy is on the upper back wall of the store, behind the large Krispy Treat display.

Hint 38: Goofy, Mickey Mouse, Pluto, and other characters are in the light brown upper wall mural around the store.

Hint 39: Classic Mickey circles are in the design in the middle of the side window that faces the lagoon.

- *Mickey's Mart* — a.k.a. *"Everything Ten Dollars and under"*

Hint 40: Above an entry door (not the lagoon side), classic Mickeys are in the upper corners.

- Marketplace Carrousel

Hint 41: At least four classic Mickeys are on the decorative panels on the Carrousel near Disney's Days of Christmas store: (1) a blue classic Mickey on the sign under Minnie Mouse, (2) two light green classic Mickeys on the dragon's nose, (3) two tiny classic Mickeys on the pink window awnings on the right side of the panel that shows part of the store from a distance, (4) pink classic Mickeys formed of roses in the upper part of the panels in the center of the Carrousel.

- Mickey's Pantry

Hint 42: You'll find classic Mickeys of different sizes and colors in the wall decorations around the store.

- Once Upon A Toy

Hint 43: In the interactive flat fountain near the Once Upon A Toy store, water tube heads are shaped like classic Mickeys, recessed lights in the cement are arranged in a classic Mickey shape, and the fountain water collects into a huge classic Mickey on the cement!

Hint 44: Outside the store, you'll find several classic Mickeys in the cement near the side entrance.

Hint 45: In a window display near the side entrance, snowflakes contain both classic and full-length Hidden Mickeys along with other Hidden Characters.

Hint 46: Outside the store's main entrance, classic Mickeys are formed by truck tires (the ears) atop Lincoln Logs.

Hint 47: A full-bodied Mickey is on a watch that hangs under an "ear" of one of the classic Mickey-shaped pincers that holds several boxes.

Hint 48: Tinker Toys on top of merchandise stands around the store form classic Mickeys.

Hint 49: At the bottom of these merchandise stands, you'll find classic Mickey supports.

Hint 50: The centers of the upper beams on wooden merchandise displays sport classic Mickey shapes.

Hint 51: Also on the wooden merchandise displays, large wing nuts on some of the bolts form Mickey ears.

Hint 52: Two black classic Mickeys are on blue sandals on one of the Mr. Potato Heads in the first room.

Hint 53: In this same room, the mural behind a service desk includes a classic Mickey balloon.

Hint 54: In a central room of the store, a classic Mickey cloud appears in a window in a mural behind the service desk.

Hint 55: In the same room, a partial classic Mickey shadow is at the top of a wall mural, to the left of the classic Mickey cloud and above a checkout counter.

Hint 56: In the next to last room, a bear with a cap that says "Disney Bear" sits in a train. He has classic Mickey buttons on his overalls.

Hint 57: In the rear room, lollipops are arranged to form classic Mickeys on the outside of the castle and merchandise stands.

- Disney's Pin Traders

Hint 58: On the large statue of Mickey and Minnie, Mickey wears a classic Mickey pin on his tie.

- Team Mickey Athletic Club

Hint 59: Outside the entrance to Team Mickey, you'll find a classic Mickey repeated in the white picket fence bordering the Disney Vacation Club display.

Hint 60: Classic Mickeys are on the bases and tops of the outside pillars.

Hint 61: Some of the mannequin heads and merchandise stands inside the store are topped with classic Mickeys, with a basketball for the head and a baseball and a tennis ball for the ears.

Hint 62: Above the monitor with golf clubs on both sides of the screen is a classic Mickey with a baseball as the head and two golf balls as the ears.

- Ghirardelli Ice Cream and Chocolate Shop

Hint 63: A classic Mickey is in the ironwork to the left of the side entrance to the shop, near the seating area.

Hint 64: A dark side-profile image of Mickey looking to the left appears as a shadow in a painting on a rear wall of the shop (to the left as you enter). Look for a streetcar in the painting. The shadow is in the streetcar's second window from the left.

- Near the lake

Hint 65: Green chairs with classic Mickeys on top are scattered around outside in the Marketplace and near the Ghirardelli shop.

Hint 66: Several sections of the green fence around the lake have repeating classic Mickeys near the top of the railing.

- World of Disney

Hint 67: Blue classic Mickeys are at the ends of the World of Disney entrance signs.

Hint 68: Light brown classic Mickeys can be found near the tops of the columns outside the store.

Hint 69: A map with continents shaped like Goofy, Donald, Pluto, and Mickey is displayed in an outside window of the Adventure Room.

Hint 70: In the Pirates outside window display, a rat with golden Mickey ears sits in a cup atop the treasures.

Hint 71: Classic Mickey holes are drilled in some of the metal posts that hold up clothing racks.

Hint 72: Some of the indoor signs for the various store sections have Mickey and other character images.

Hint 73: In the Adventure and Pirate room, at least three classic Mickey-shaped images are on a map along the front of the cashier's counter.

Hint 74: In the high-ceilinged central room, behind the three little pigs floating overhead, a wall mural has a classic Mickey emblem above the doors of the Chinese Theater.

Hint 75: In the same room, the Pocahontas airship has an upside-down classic Mickey at the very bottom of the rear vertical tail fin, near where the tail fin connects to the body of the airship.

Hint 76: In the same room, you'll find a classic Mickey on a flag in the background of the Tweedle Dee and Tweedle Dum wall mural.

Hint 77: That mural also includes a classic Mickey on Tweedle Dee's apron.

Hint 78: In the same room of the store, some of the female mannequins have classic Mickey freckles under their eyes.

Hint 79: On the walls in the central Genie Room, blue classic Mickeys can be spotted in the compass paintings.

Hint 80: Subtle classic Mickeys hide in the red wallpaper of the Genie Room's display cabinets. Change your angle of view if you have trouble spotting them.

Hint 81: Also on the Genie Room walls, antique-looking maps on wood panels painted to look like tapestries have land masses that resemble the side profiles of Mickey

Mouse, Winnie the Pooh, Goofy, and possibly Donald Duck. (Donald is a bit of a stretch.)

Hint 82: On the wall in the Villain Room, next door to the Genie Room, Cruella DeVille's left wrist is wrapped with fur that has a classic Mickey dark spot on the side.

Hint 83: Near the World of Disney store, in an entrance to Downtown Disney from the parking lot, three pots form a classic Mickey fountain.

- LEGO Imagination Center

Hint 84: Outside the store is a family made of LEGOS. One of their dogs is a Dalmatian with black spots that form a classic Mickey.

- T-Rex Café

Hint 85: Just inside the entrance and over the bar, a pink classic Mickey is on the body of an octopus across from a green praying mantis.

WDW Casting Center

Hint 86: Classic Mickey holes are in the upper outside walls of the Casting building. (These Hidden Mickeys can also be spotted from Interstate 4.)

WDW Miniature Golf Courses

- Fantasia Gardens

Hint 87: The tee-off areas on both courses are marked with classic Mickeys.

Hint 88: On the Gardens Course, the green at the 12th hole is shaped like a classic Mickey.

- Winter Summerland

Hint 89: On the third hole of the Winter Course, candy canes, milk, and gingerbread men pop out of "Defrosty the cooler." One is a gingerbread cookie featuring Mickey ears.

235

Hint 90: On the 16th hole of the Winter Course, you'll find Goofy and Donald nutcrackers on the left side of the mantelpiece.

Hint 91: A Mickey Mouse gingerbread cookie pokes out from a stocking hanging on the right side of the same mantelpiece.

Hint 92: On the left side of the 16th hole of the Summer Course, Mickey and Minnie Mouse are sitting in a sleigh on the mantelpiece, along with Pluto. Since the 16th holes of both courses are close together, this mantelpiece is also visible from the 16th and 17th holes of the Winter Course.

Near Celebration, Florida

Hint 93: On the west side of Interstate 4, south of exit 62 near Celebration, you'll find a huge classic Mickey atop an electrical transmission line pole.

Near the Magic Kingdom

Hint 94: A few miles northwest of the Magic Kingdom, a huge green classic Mickey made of groves of trees can only be seen from the air (or on a Google image). The Hidden Mickey is in a field just off Highway 27 and near the 192 merge.

Other Mickey Appearances

These Hidden Mickeys won't earn you any points, but you're bound to enjoy them if you're in the right place at the right time to see them.

★ Look for holiday Hidden Mickeys if you're at Walt Disney World during the Christmas season or any major holiday. For example, the "Osborne Family Spectacle of Lights" along the backlot area at Disney's Hollywood Studios includes many hiding Mickeys.

★ Other "Hidden" Mickeys — décor and deliberate — appear with some regularity throughout WDW. Notice the Mickster on WDW brochures, maps and flags, Cast Member nametags, guest room keys, pay telephones and phone books, and restaurant and store receipts. The restaurants sometimes offer classic Mickey butter and margarine pats, pancakes and waffles, pizzas and pasta, as well as Mickeys on napkins and food trays. They also arrange dishes and condiments to form classic Mickeys, and some condiment containers are shaped like Mickey.

The Mickey hat and ears on top of the "Earful Tower" are obvious to every visitor in the vicinity of Disney's Hollywood Studios. Many road signs on WDW Resort property sport Mickey ears, and WDW vehicles and monorails have Mickey Mouse images and insignia.

Cleaning personnel will often spray the ground, windows, furniture, and other items with three circles of cleaning solution (a classic Mickey) before the final cleansing. Or they may leave three wet Mickey Mouse circles on the pavement after mopping! Mickey even decorates manhole covers, survey markers, and utility covers in the ground, as you've had a chance to find out for yourself on some of the scavenger hunts.

Enjoy all these Mickeys as you explore WDW. And if you want to take some home with you, rest assured that you can always find "Hidden" Mickeys on souvenir mugs, merchandise bags and boxes, T-shirts, and Christmas tree ornaments sold in the Disney World shops. So even when you're far away from WDW, you can continue to enjoy Hidden Mickeys.

CHAPTER 9

My Favorite Hidden Mickeys

●●●●●●●●●●●●●●●●●●●●●●●●●●●

In this book, I've described over 800 Hidden Mickeys at Walt Disney World. I enjoy every one of them, but the following are extra special to me. They're special because of their uniqueness, their deep camouflage (which makes them especially hard to find), or the "Eureka!" response they elicit when I spot them — or any combination of the above. Here then are my Top Ten Hidden Mickeys and, not far behind, Ten Honorable Mentions. I apologize to you if your favorite Hidden Mickey is not (yet) on the lists below.

My Top Ten

1. Mickey hiding behind the fern on the big mural inside the Garden Grill restaurant, The Land Pavilion, Epcot. When I outline this Mickey (a Cast Member often hands me a broom to reach it), I have witnessed folks in the restaurant smile and shout, "I see him; look, there's Mickey!"

2. The "waving Mickey" just past the tiger exhibit, *Maharajah Jungle Trek*, Asia, Disney's Animal Kingdom. If you can find him, wave back for good luck!

3. Minnie Mouse's shadow on the mural by the loading dock, *The Great Movie Ride*, Disney's Hollywood Studios. Once you see her, you'll never forget her.

4. Mickey peeking out of a hole in an overhead beam in the lobby of the Wilderness Lodge Villas. Outstanding effect!

5. Mickey in the vines outside the rear lobby doors, Animal Kingdom Lodge Resort. Hard to find, fun to spot.

6. Mickey sitting on the edge of the roof of a building next to the Contemporary

Resort. This playful Mickey welcomes you to the Magic Kingdom.

7. The "Grim Reaper" Mickey, *The Haunted Mansion*, Liberty Square, Magic Kingdom. A classic.

8. The golf ball Mickey, *Soarin'*, Future World, Epcot. Don't blink, or you'll miss this Mickey!

9. Mickey in rocks, Japan Pavilion, World Showcase, Epcot. One of the best rock Mickeys anywhere.

10. Mickey sitting with Donald on the wall, "Raiders of the Lost Ark" scene, *The Great Movie Ride*, Disney's Hollywood Studios. A real regal Mickey.

Ten Honorable Mentions

1. Mickey in the rafters in The Milk House (the Field House), Disney's Wide World of Sports. The Main Mouse benevolently watches over his minions.

2. The tree grove classic Mickey a few miles northwest of the Magic Kingdom. You can only see it from the air or on a Google image. A real special "Hidden" Mickey!

3. An image of Mickey traced in the tile near the rear parking lot, Contemporary Resort. It's worth the trip to marvel at this amazing Mickey.

4. Mickey on the wall along the entrance queue near the faux fireplace, *Pirates of the Caribbean*, Adventureland, Magic Kingdom. Squint to spot this Mickey; you'll never forget him!

5. The side profile of Mickey on the tree at the *Swiss Family Treehouse*, Adventureland, Magic Kingdom. One of the very best side-profile Mickeys.

6. The utility cover classic Mickey by the Tamu Tamu Refreshment Shop, Africa, Disney's Animal Kingdom. The mundane utility cover transformed.

7. The huge Hidden Jafar along the *Pangani Forest Exploration Trail*, Africa, Disney's Animal Kingdom. The sight will take your breath away.

8. The classic Mickey in the cement behind Mouse Gear Shop, Future World, Epcot. Tiny and remarkable. A child found it first!

9. A dark green classic Mickey set of leaves on a wall just past the tiger exhibit, *Maharajah Jungle Trek*, Asia, Disney's Animal Kingdom. Well hidden, hard to find, a beautiful classic Mickey.

10. Minnie Moo, with her black classic Mickey marking, is back! She's in a photograph hanging in the Yachtsman Steakhouse, Yacht Club Resort. Pay your respects to this one-of-a-kind Disney icon.

CHAPTER 10

Don't Stop Now!

Hidden Mickey mania is contagious. The benign pastime of searching out Hidden Mickeys has escalated into a bona fide vacation mission for many Walt Disney World fans. I'm proud to include my name among them. Searching for images of the Main Mouse can enhance a solo trip to the parks or a vacation for the entire family. Little ones delight in spotting and greeting Mickey Mouse characters in the parks and restaurants. As children grow, the Hidden Mickey game is a natural evolution of their fondness for the Mouse.

Join the search! With alert eyes and mind, you can spot Hidden Mickey classics and new ones waiting to be found. Even beginners have happened upon a new, unreported Hidden Mickey or two. As new attractions open and older ones get refurbished, new Hidden Mickeys await discovery.

It may be just my imagination but I swear that every time I visit Walt Disney World, I spot a Hidden Mickey up in the clouds, watching over his domain! Do you think the Imagineers might actually have some influence on the atmosphere over Walt Disney World?

The Disney entertainment phenomenon is unique in many ways, and Hidden Mickey mania is one manifestation of Disney's universal appeal. Join in the fun! Maybe I'll see you at Walt Disney World, marveling (like me) at the Hidden Gems. They're waiting patiently for you to discover them.

Index to Mickey's Hiding Places

Note: This Index includes only those rides, restaurants, hotels, and other places and attractions that harbor confirmed Hidden Mickeys. So if the attraction you're looking for isn't included, Mickey isn't hiding there. Or if he is, I haven't yet spotted him. – *Steve Barrett*

The following abbreviations appear in this Index:

AK	-	Disney's Animal Kingdom
DD	-	Downtown Disney
DH	-	Disney's Hollywood Studios
E	-	Epcot
MK	-	Magic Kingdom
R	-	Located in a Resort hotel complex
WP	-	Water Park

M